LONDON'S GREATEST GRAND HOTELS

LONDON'S GREATEST GRAND HOTELS

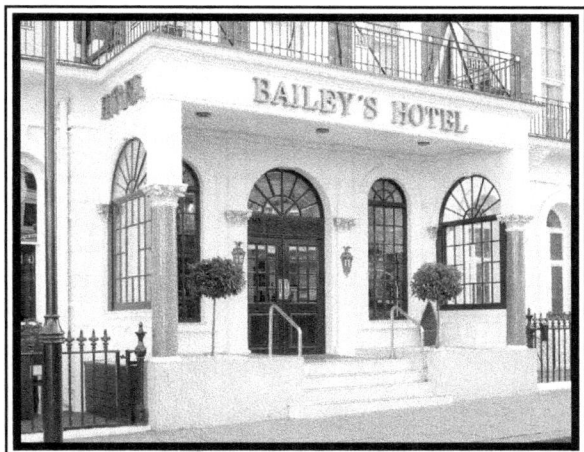

Extraordinary People, Extraordinary Service in the World's Cultural Capital

WARD MOREHOUSE III
& KATHERINE BOYNTON

Thousand Islands Productions Inc.
New York, New York

Thousand Islands Productions Inc.
in association with BearManor Media presents:

London's Greatest Grand Hotels
Extraordinary People, Extraordinary Service
in the World's Cultural Capital

For information:
BearManor Media
P.O. Box 1129
Duncan, OK 73534-1129

www.BearManorMedia.com

Cover & book design by
Bob Antler, Antler Designworks

ISBN: 978-1-62933-075-4
Printed in the USA

For Will Morehouse,
the Boynton Family—Liz, King, John and Paloma
and for Rod & Katy Rahe who love to travel.

CONTENTS

PREFACE

This book, London's Greatest Grand Hotels, is a new and highly subjective sequel of London's Grand Hotels, published in 2010. There have been a number of changes in London hotel life since I wrote about it and I've brought in a collaborator — my new wife. *London's Greatest Grand Hotels* includes brand new chapters on The Ham Yard, Chelsea Harbour Hotel, Café Royal, The Langham and Queen Mary 2, as well as expanded chapters on Millennium Mayfair, The Savoy and Lanesborough.

— Ward Morehouse III

It's been a privilege to write about many of London's Greatest Grand Hotels. In this book, the first person refers to Ward. He draws on years of his rich historical hotel experience. Where there is an entry specific to me, it is noted accordingly. Otherwise "we" is used since we traveled and had interviews in London together beginning in 2014. In this book there are eight hotels I've written about. They are: Bailey's Hotel, Millennium Mayfair, The Chelsea Harbor, Hotel Café Royal, Ham Yard Hotel, The Savoy Hotel, Langham Hotel and Queen Mary 2.

To me luxury in its highest sense is a spiritual idea. Service too. When I realized this my life opened up in new beautiful ways, before I met my husband. He coming into it and being asked to write about these hotels has shown me more about this sweet truth.

—Katherine Boynton

BAILEY'S HOTEL

"Bailey's Hotel has a warm, classical elegance. We are greeted like royalty by the ebony staircase gracefully descending into the grand lobby. The lobby's arch of crimson carpet and gold accents make me wonder … perhaps I am the Queen today? Above me is a jeweled chandelier that catches light like morning stars. Sarah, the concierge, offers a warm greeting from behind the front desk. Even the redolent, nearby purple orchids appear to wave hello. Sarah's golden hair and smile match her spirit, which is like the sun. She seems to radiate and anticipate my needs before I ask. Offering an immediate room to rest from the long night of travel, even when arriving so early. I feel safe, comfortable, and at home.

"I'm revived quickly when staying at Bailey's. Thanks to the delicious and healthy food at Olives, their Italian restaurant that's filled with hotel guests as well as those from the bustling Kensington neighborhood. And what a neighborhood it is! Full of life, little shops, and a short jog to Kensington Gardens. As I ventured out to explore the storybook streets, the heel came off my boot. It was my first day in London with two weeks of travel ahead. Sarah, of course, was there to solve the impossible; my boot was given to her that night and was returned to my door the next morning as good as new.

"A soothing ending to an evening is found at Bailey's Hotel in Olives Restaurant. The white chocolate and lavender crème brulee is something all artists or those who love fine perfume should experience."

—Katherine Boynton

Bailey's has remained open during its recent renovation. It's an "eight-month 'rolling' refurbishment (a lot of rooms will remain open) so we're not closing the hotel," explained Clive Harrington as we sat for breakfast at Bailey's.

Millennium Hotels' own history of Bailey's, which it commissioned, pretty much tells it like it was, and is, and we are tacking fairly close to their official account in the following description.

First and foremost, Bailey's is one of the oldest hotels in London still standing, and operating. Moreover, like many a refined and beautiful London lady, it has a fascinating history. Unlike most London ladies, the hotel's history stretches back to 1876. Perhaps not too surprisingly the story of the hotel begins with a gentleman by the name of the Right Honourable Sir James Bailey, MP, who was born in 1840 and died in 1910. Among his many other remarkable achievements in life during the better part of the Victorian age, Mr. Bailey was the original owner of the hotel which came to bear his name. Mr. Bailey and his hotel are also inseparable from the history of the particular section of Kensington which houses the hotel. Mr. Bailey's hotel, through ingenuity, luck and much hard work managed to survive not only the turn of the century, and the unfortunate death of Mr. Bailey, but two world wars, subsequent changes in ownership and at least one serious threat of demolition. Frankly, given all this turmoil of over one and a quarter centuries, it is practically amazing that the hotel has managed to hang on to its original structure. Someone who stayed there in the 1870s probably wouldn't even have any trouble recognizing the place today, assuming that person was extremely long-lived, that is. The hotel in fact is in itself a fairly important London architectural landmark, and not simply as a result of its longevity and tenacity. The hotel is one of the defining characteristics of its unique neighborhood, Kensington.

One of the important things to remember about London is that it really is not one city but a number of neighboring towns that sort of grew together over the centuries. In fact, London only recently got her first mayor. Even as late as the 19th century, Westminster was really a different place than Kensington. This is one of the reasons why many of the areas of Greater London have such different, and distinct, characters. Take for example the advertisement that James Bailey himself employed to promote his hotel in its earlier days, in which he referred to Kensington as "the healthiest and most fashionable part of London." Anyone who has read Dickens or any of the other great English novelists of the 18th and 19th centuries knows full well that there were, alas, certain sections of town which were distinctly unhealthy. Plumbing, remember, was itself once a luxury. Kensington, being somewhat removed from the more congested central parts of the city, was practically out in the country in James Bailey's day. However, more important to the hotel's purposes, it was situated in a section that was more likely to attract London's aristocrats and the more successful members of that new, upwardly mobile class—the bourgeoisie. In short, rich people. Kensington had one other attractive quality for the Right Honourable owner and that was the relative scarcity of nearby hotels at the time of its founding. James Bailey had the local upper class market to himself. Better still, the area, while removed from the trouble spots, was nonetheless close enough to the city's main attractions and social and business centers. Why, it even had a brand new "underground railway" that could zip hotel guests to central London in as little as five minutes, as well as to "all parts of London." No doubt, even the swells liked to use the underground when it was new. Mr. Bailey's hotel was also conveniently situated near the Royal Albert Hall, Hyde Park, the National History Museum, and the Royal Horticultural and Kensington Gardens. And for those guests who wished not to descend underground to get around, the original hotel boasted no fewer than nine stables, which housed "well-appointed" carriages to convey guests to wherever lay their heart's desire. No ratty dog carts for these folks!

It's very interesting to read in the hotel's history that there were actually very few hotels, as such, in all of London at this time. And the aim of James Bailey in constructing his hotel was to provide accommodations on par with the local royal establishments or, at least, to be "not inferior to Buckingham Palace, Buckingham Gate." Thanks to changes in the social order and to the Industrial Revolution, there was now apparently a need to suitably house the town's nouveau riche, as well as its old rich. The colorful travelers' inns and boarding houses just would no longer suffice.

As for James Bailey's own personal history, he was the son of William Bailey, who was a farmer in Mattishall, Norfolk. James did not, it seems, take to farming life as he absconded early in life for London. Not that he entirely turned his back on Mattishall, but clearly he was an ambitious young fellow. When he made his fortune in the capital, he did donate a beautiful organ to his local parish church in Mattishall.

It is unknown, however, what exactly prompted James Bailey to head for London at the age of twenty, which was in the year 1860. Rumor has it that he began his professional life as a butler shortly after arrival. This, remember, was a time when a large household, not to mention a palace or a hotel, required an enormous amount of daily labor. Not only was there no electricity, there were really none of the labor-saving devices we so take for granted today. Everything depended on two types of power-horse power and human sweat. It is known that, at some later date, James Bailey managed to acquire the Harrington Hotel, which like Bailey's is also located in Gloucester Road. As bright as he was hardworking, Bailey enlarged his new purchase, a practice he would continue when he constructed the future Bailey's itself. What everyone at Bailey's today would love to know about their progenitor is just how he managed to finance these considerable purchases - on a butler's salary! Which, in those days, could not have been very considerable. Presumably, he was also something of a financial wizard. Or extremely frugal! Most likely, he used his good name and managed to borrow the money, then made good on it.

One of the few things the remarkable Mr. Bailey did not do all by himself was actually build the structure of Bailey's Hotel. A well-known property owner by the name of H. B. Alexander, it seems, arranged the construction of the hotel with the assistance of the developers Charles Aldin, Jr. and William Aldin. The Aldins were quite well known in the Kensington area at this time, and had developed many other projects,

including James Bailey's first hotel, the Harrington Hotel at 25 Gloucester Road. (Of course, this does raise the question of who was Mr. Harrington?) The Aldins, busy as bees, also built the houses and shops
which surrounded Mr. Bailey's new hotel. Indeed, it must have been a
most prosperous time, in Kensington at any rate. The name of the actual
architect of the hotel is unknown, even though in that day this must have
been a construction project that created what we in this day would call
serious buzz. On the other hand, architects were not the celebrities then
that they are now, so this anonymity is perhaps not so peculiar.

Whoever the fellow was, his design began a new architectural fashion in Kensington. Before Bailey's went up, the neighborhood was pop-
ulated with buildings that had fronts, according to the *London Survey*,
of "White Ipswich, Suffolk, Gault or Beart's patent bricks." We have
no idea what any of that is, but it certainly doesn't sound too attractive.
James Bailey's new hotel, on the other hand, was constructed with red
bricks with "white dressings of Bath stone." The upshot was that red
brick became a viable building material for swanky addresses. Overall,
the hotel conforms to most other fashions of the Victorian age, but this
red-and-white bricks effect became a distinguishing characteristic of
Kensington and has lasted to the current day. Not too surprisingly, since
it is most appealing.

If you, as an American, were confused enough at the British call-
ing elevators "lifts," what would you have made of the Bailey's Hotel's
brand new "ascending rooms?" True, they were just simple elevators,
but the term "ascending room" still conjures up for us the image of an
entire hotel room that goes up and down. The new building also boasted
a "safe room," which also sounds quite intriguing, but which, again,
simply referred to a metal safe. More important still, there were bathrooms on every floor. This was quite the luxury back then, when private
baths were practically unheard of, even in the great houses and palaces.
The luxurious "bath room" is a fairly modern concept. Back then, they
were just privies and closets with tubs in them. Very utilitarian.

Apparently, Bailey's was a big international hit from the moment it
opened its doors. At least we know that the great American author of,
among other things, "The Luck of Roaring Camp," Bret Harte checked

in during the first year of operation. Also, Eduard Strauss, the younger brother of the more renowned Austrian composer Johann Strauss, stopped by about the same time. More importantly to Mr. Bailey's bottom line, British royals flocked to its spectacular Victorian grand ballroom. Bailey's had arrived!

James Bailey himself did not reside in his beautiful new hotel. He'd bought 4 Harrington Gardens nearby for his private home. At this time he also owned the South Kensington Hotel in Queensgate Terrace, so he was becoming quite the Victorian Age real estate mogul. Then, in 1877, Mr. B built up Bailey's down Courtfield Road with extensions and, in 1881, those nine stables were leveled to make room for a garden and other extensions. Today, this area is home to the Bombay Brasserie. Not yet ready to rest on his laurels, Mr. B had new bedrooms installed in 1883 and, in 1890, a new elevator system and electric lights in all the rooms. This was quite forward thinking. Many people at that time still thought electric lights were dangerous. (Actually, Edison's rather clumsy DC current was prone to killing the odd horse in the street that had the misfortune to step on the buried cable.)

By this time Bailey's Hotel had grown to over 300 rooms and even Mr. B could no longer resist not living there — he'd moved himself and his entire family into the place. To make life easier for Mr. B, the hotel also served as domicile to about thirty-five of the staff members, helping to serve the customers better. Bailey's was becoming quite the tight-knit little hospitality community. You know you like your boss when you live in the same house with him. Especially if it's possible he might ring you up for room service at two in the morning.

Despite the expense and trouble to cross the Atlantic in this era (don't forget, the Titanic disaster wasn't until 1912), America and Britain may have been closer then than they are now — at least culturally. In any case, many of Bailey's early customers were Americans, both on business and pleasure trips. The *Survey of London* tellingly quotes a tourist guide of the era (1891, to be precise), commending Bailey's Hotel for its "cozy, homelike atmosphere, which is enhanced by rich and substantial surroundings." Sounds like at least a four-star recommendation. The guide went on to commend the wine, too, as well as the sanitary arrangements and, a little more peculiar to us in this age, the fire. Remember, back then before central heating, the fireplace in your room was much more than decorative. In fact, this is probably why the luxurious private bath took so long to come along — bing) and then, when the only really warm room was one with a roaring fireplace. Ah, but we take so much for granted these days.

After all this whirlwind of activity, James Bailey in the 1890s would grow somewhat tired of the hotel business. First he sold off both of his hotels to Spiers and Pond Limited in 1894. Probably this change of heart was due to his newly booming career as a London official. He served at this time on the boards of Harrods and D. H. Evans — both world famous department stores, only the former not quite as much as the latter. Then in 1895 Mr. B was elected a Member of Parliament for the Walworth division of Newington, a post he would hold onto until 1906. He also busied himself as a Kensington vestryman from 1878 to 1894, as Deputy Lieutenant for Norfolk, and as a Justice of the Peace in Essex. As you can see, his energy had not dwindled in the slightest. Oh, yes, a vestryman is a member of a local church's operational body, or vestry. Mr. B with all that extra time still on his hands was also a founding member of the Constitutional Club. This doesn't surprise. Obviously, the Club was open only to gentlemen with iron constitutions like Mr. B's. For all this selfless, endless service, Mr. B was at last knighted in 1905, and five years later he died at his home in Rutland Gate. He left an estate of 245,000 pounds sterling, which even now is a heck of a lot of dough. But no wonder, really. He was so darn busy his whole life he probably never had a free moment in which to spend a farthing.

We sadly leave Mr. Bailey but his hotel goes gloriously on without him.

When first erected, the hotel had virtually no competition in the area, but this changed by 1914, when there were no fewer than fourteen hotels in eighteen buildings, all situated in Cromwell Road and Harrington Gardens which, if you're keeping score at home, is the area roughly south of the southwest corner of Hyde Park. Not surprisingly, this phenomenal growth in the London hospitality industry tailed off at the start of the First World War. But it also changed very little in the years between the two World Wars. (There was a little event going on at the time called a worldwide Depression.) But, by 1939, the start of the Second World War, a major part of the Kensington area had been purchased with plans to build numerous new hotels. Many of these, however, were merely houses converted to use as hotels, unlike Bailey's which had been designed and built from scratch as a luxury guest establishment. In short, the new competition was not, pleasant as they no doubt were, that intimidating custom-wise.

You may have heard or read about the inconveniences much of the city of London suffered at the hands of the Luftwaffe during WWII. Well, Bailey's did not, alas, pass through the conflict without its share of nicks and scrapes. In fact, in October of 1940, an incendiary bomb hit it square on, starting a major fire and causing, of course, much damage to the hotel's building. Some of this war damage would not be repaired until the early Fifties. The last to be reinstated were the badly damaged fourth and fifth floors. The hotel was not open during the whole of the war. The hotel's records here are a little incomplete, but it is believed the hotel served as a provisional hospital or even a shelter. Now that's what I call waiting out the war in style! None of these dingy tube stations for me! I want the ambassador suite, please! You don't suppose there was room service available during the blitz, do you? Probably not. Even the fabled English hospitality has its limits, after all.

In 1945, the hotel suffered again with a fire in the staff quarters. Ceilings and floorboards were damaged and the entire hotel was evacuated. The structure, however, was not threatened, thank goodness. During the early Fifties, rather extensive alterations were carried out on the hotel, in fact. New bathrooms were installed in 1954, for instance. (It must be very hard for hotels to keep pace with bathroom technology; must cost a fortune to keep installing those newfangled fixtures. After all, a bed is a bed. A chair a chair. But every few years, showers and tubs keep getting ritzier and ritzier.) The new owners were not satisfied, however, and at the end of the Fifties, they made further major alterations, the highlight of which was a brand new bar. By now they must have had all their customers covered — those who check in and want nothing but a nice hot bath, and those who check in and want nothing but a nice chilled cocktail.

Despite all this new activity, however, the hotel actually came under the threat of demolition at about this same time. The Royal Borough of Kensington and Chelsea rode to the rescue, declaring that it would deeply regret such a loss to the neighborhood, arguing that the hotel forms an integral part of the area because of its historical value. Hear, hear! Disaster was indeed averted. There have, though, been many changeovers in management and ownership since Mr. B was laid to rest. In 1988, for instance, Bailey's was completely restored before it was taken over from the Taj Group by Securum Hotel Holdings (the actual transaction took place in 1992). Only a couple of years later, in 1994, the hotel was then acquired by City Developments Limited (CDL).

Never fear, however, despite all this financial finagling as well as two world wars, Bailey's has maintained most of its original structure. The original main hall is almost untouched, with its large marble pillars, grand staircase, stained glass windows, and Victorian plasterwork. Today, Bailey's is a four-star hotel with 211 rooms and has not relinquished one iota of its prestige. Of course, beautiful old pillars are lovely to look at, but a modern hotel has to change with the times and all of the rooms offer all the modern conveniences in addition to the great cultural and architectural history. The cost of a room has also changed somewhat since Mr. B built his beautiful hotel. In the 1890s, rooms supposedly went for a dollar a night for a single. Perhaps more surprisingly, by the 1970s that had gone up to only twelve pounds a night. By 1986 the cost had hit forty pounds and by the present millennium, about 145 pounds. It makes one wonder if Mr. H. G. Wells' time machine is still available in London. The use of it for even one night could save you a bundle on a hotel stay. On the other hand, they didn't have Wi-Fi in 1890. What they did have back then was once described as "homelike atmosphere which is enhanced by the rich and substantial surroundings." Moreover, the site that the prescient Mr. B chose is still a propitious one for a hotel, still not too close and not too far from most of what one wishes to visit in town. Needless to say, the service at the hotel has never suffered a setback and the atmosphere of both the hotel and Kensington are as sanguine as ever. In short, the hotel still has all that made it so attractive to guests for over a hundred years, in addition to the Wi-Fi and all the other modern conveniences. At Bailey's, as at so many of the great luxury London hotels, a traveler truly is getting the best of both worlds, the past and the present.

Unlike many hotels in America, room service is an ongoing, honored tradition at Bailey's. Even the night room service menu (10:30 p.m. to 7 a.m.) is excellent. A rich Spaghetti Bolognese is £13.50 and there is an "exotic fruit salad" for £6.00.

"A little secret: Bailey's just may be my favorite hotel in London."
—Ward Morehouse III

People from all walks of life and classes come to Bailey's, like someone slipping into a favorite pair of slippers or leather shoes. When Bailey's opened in 1876, Kensington had virtually no other hotels. Even in 1876, the Gloucester Road underground tube station had trains leaving every five minutes "for all parts of London," advertisements said. As such it was an area very much like Times Square at the dawn of the 20th century when subway lines converged on Times Square, so-called because of the New York Times building dominating the pre-skyscraper skyline. Of course, times as well as costs have changed even though Kensington, close to magnificent Hyde Park, Royal Albert Hall and the Natural History Museum, has blossomed even more since 1876.

Bailey's Hotel just feels like home. To be sure, who can resist the gilt-edge London Ritz with perhaps the most gorgeous high tea in the world, or the views of the Thames from a suite at The Savoy or The Chelsea Harbor Hotels. (Claude Monet stayed at The Savoy, closer to the center of town, when he painted the Thames.) But Bailey's, dating back to 1876 in Kensington, which James Bailey, who built the hotel, called "the healthiest and most fashionable part of London," is a place any of us—authors, readers, stars, tourists—would find delightful.

"Chairman Kwek hand picks all of us for his hotel," said the manager I interviewed on our visit. "I've got a love for the old building as well, and for the customs of it. And certainly for the Bailey's. And once you start getting involved with James Bailey,

20

and his reason for building it, you start delving into his life. You fall in love with the hotel. It's a rags-to-riches story, a farmer's son from Northampton coming to London from Northampton, becoming a butler. Getting a little bit of money together and putting his first boarding house together. Educating himself and molding himself into a gentleman.

"Then he was knighted and became Sir James Bailey, the first M.P. to be on the Board of Harrods as well. And later being on a planning board for the Gloucester Road tube station.

"James Bailey lived at the hotel for some time, in the front part of Bailey's. "And when you know about the man you can start seeing some of the bits and pieces that are unique about the hotel," the manager added.

"In the U.K. we had our unique form of Prohibition, which is why the Bailey's front bar is one of the first gin palaces in this part of London as well. It had to be licensed to do that (to serve gin). There were only four licenses provided for, and looking forward to its renovation we're converting the bar back into a gin palace. And that's becoming a very sexy thing in London at the moment: cocktail bars, gin palaces. The fact we were a gin palace makes it doubly as special going forward. So we're excited about that. So just re-branding her and giving her back a bit of a classic feel.

"Kensington is even today, from a real estate point of view, more valuable than Mayfair. And certainly income per household is much more than Mayfair. It's considered the second wealthiest suburb in Europe which is why Olives Restaurant does so well. When you can get the proper balance between hotel guests and people from the neighborhood, you've got a winner. … It's a great restaurant.

"It's not a bed factory, as Clive Harrington was saying, because often a hotel allocates you a room. They don't care who's arriving, where the booking is coming from, that kind of thing.

"We look at where they're arriving from, their geographic location, and we can pinpoint what room is best for them.

"In the refurbishment in 1946, it was discovered that the hotel had quite extensive bomb damage during the Second World War and that had never been (completely) rectified. The Luftwaffe was looking for transportation links to bomb.

"For leisure guests who are looking to see and explore London this is the place."

Our grand tour continued its spectacular grandness next at the Millennium Bailey's Hotel — located at 140 Gloucester Road in the heart of fashionable Kensington, less than a minute's walk from Gloucester Road tube station (that's London lingo for subway station for those of you new to "Britishisms").

Bailey's is an undiscovered London treasure. We spent nearly a week at the hotel and loved every minute, from the almost suite-sized single room to the ambiance, location and ultra-friendly staff.

Feeling more like a Victorian townhouse than a hotel, Bailey's suggests New York's historic Algonquin Hotel. Its authentic Victorian decor with sweeping staircases and real fireplaces exudes nostalgia. *Vive la difference* between Bailey's and the adjoining Millennium Gloucester Hotel. A full-service, felicitous "convention hotel" with ball and function rooms, it would be at home in the New York Hilton or Sheraton Center. Yet, as sleek and modern as it is, it boasts the Bombay Brasserie, London's finest Indian restaurant.

The hotel's conference center (known as the Millennium Conference Center), which interconnects the Bailey's and the Millennium Gloucester, seems big enough for an auto show, which it has been used for! Its promotion profile states: "Our venue offers a choice of twenty-five versatile conferencing and banqueting suites, suitable for both business and social functions and capable of accommodating two to 500 delegates. About 17,000 sq. ft. of meeting and event space have been carefully re-designed and refurbished to provide total flexibility along with state-of-the-art technical equipment including 10 mb uncontested SDSL broadband, Wi-Fi, screening facilities and intelligent lighting. The hotel also has a full civil wedding ceremony license for all of its rooms. AV equipment is also available for hire and a dedicated staff will be on-hand for your event." We love that full civil wedding license point, the way it's slipped in there among all the other amenities, like having your shoes shined. To top this off, combining both the Bailey's and Gloucester hotels, their facilities can offer some 820 rooms, making them one of the most expansive facilities which can hold world-class conferences, conventions and meetings — small and large scale.

But Millennium is not easy to position in the hotel world. Its chairman, Singapore-born and -based Kwek Leng Beng (or, as he is most commonly called, Chairman Kwek, one of the wealthiest men in the world) has a passion for history and the arts. He restored Broadway's Hudson Theatre (a subject which I wrote about in full in my book *Discovering the Hudson*) and owns The Millennium Biltmore Hotel in Los Angeles, which was "the" Oscars hotel for many years. He and his company defy traditional corporate profiles. Some of his hotels are extraordinarily modern, sleek; others notably historic, embodying the rich tapestry of old-world architecture and heritage. He seems to have not only a love and appreciation for great hotels around the world but almost a hobbyist's affection for them, like a classic car buff or stamp collector. He wants passionately to share his love of hotels not only with his guests, of course, but with all around the world. Of course, collecting beautiful hotels is not a hobby for everyone!

At the invitation of Chairman Kwek, I had the pleasure of dining at the Bugis Street Brasserie, located at the Millennium Gloucester, which adjoins the Bailey's. It offers authentic Singaporean, Malaysian and Chinese cuisine with house specialties that include *Mee Goreng* (Malay-style fried noodles) and *Nasi Goreng* (Malay-style fried rice), fish fillets stir-fried with black pepper sauce and aromatic crispy duck.

In what sounds more like a documentary film than one of the best hotelier's effort to go the extra mile, Millennium & Copthorne Hotels plc donated a grand piano to the Wai Wai, an Indian tribe in Guyana, according to an article in *Caribbean Best* in March 2001. We think this story will give insights to Chairman Kwek's unique relationship to his hotels, to people and to the world.

In a tale seemingly right out of *King Solomon's Mines*, an explorer by the name of Colonel John Blashford-Snell (honest, that's his real

23

name) had been conducting an expedition into the remote regions of equatorial Guyana, during which he came upon the minute Amerindian Wai Wai tribe and befriended them. So much so that he found himself promising to bring them back a grand piano. What did the tribe want with a piano and just how did the Colonel imagine he could physically transport such a delicate, enormous object into the jungle, are both intriguing questions. The natives dwell in the forest at the edge of the Essequibo River in the extreme south of Guyana. The Colonel had already brought the 190-member tribe much needed medical supplies, the sort of things adventurers imagine that primitive tribes would need. But, no, the Wai Wai tribe wanted a grand piano.

Apparently as the Colonel was departing the village, a priest by the name of Elessa asked him to bring back a grand piano for the tiny church there. The Colonel knew of course that the cleric was requesting the near impossible. Although it may be an occupational hazard for priests to expect the impossible, Elessa had certainly confidence in God, and also, it seems, in the Colonel.

Finding a sponsor for the grand piano back in England was the relatively easy part. As noted, Chairman Kwek's company Millennium Hotels & Resorts offered to foot the bill on the musical instrument. Meanwhile, the explorer got in touch with BWIA, who offered to transport the piano to Trinidad. After that, the explorer would have to rely on his own devices. So he and his team (and the grand piano) planned to take small planes into the Guyanese interior. Then, when that was no longer practical, they would hoof it the rest of the way back to the Wai Wai village.

But, wait. You didn't think it was going to be that easy, Colonel, did you? Just as they were leaving London (with the grand piano), they were informed by the Guyanese government that the Wai Wai had had to relocate — the entire village — because they'd been flooded out of their old neighborhood. They'd moved upriver from Akou to Masekenari. Moreover, they now urgently needed medical supplies. As well as school books and tools with which to build a whole new village.

Still undaunted, the Colonel pushed off from London with seven other members of his new expedition. In addition to the rather large grand piano, they carried a supply of medicine and the other necessities. The team arrived by small plane in Guyana's interior, 350 miles from the capital of Georgetown. Then, for three days, they lugged their cargo through the steaming jungle, crossing rope bridges, then rode by canoe the last leg of the trip up to the Wai Wai's new settlement.

Some in the group feared that the piano strings might not have survived all this damp hot weather, not to mention all the jostling. To everyone's amazement (except, no doubt, for the priest) everything was in perfect working order. The piano was uncrated in the middle of town and the villagers erupted with a cry of delight — which must have seemed to make it all worthwhile for the Colonel. Next, one of the expedition members taught several of the tribesmen how to play and care for their new instrument. Not much later, an open-air concert (the town concert hall must have been booked) was held. The Wai Wai tribe performed native songs and their own compositions.

Just think of it. Delivering a grand piano from London to the South American jungle. Now, that's what we call room service! Those top London hoteliers, they don't seem to be able to say no to anything.

MILLENNIUM MAYFAIR

~⊘ ⊘~

"Tree top views! Waking up at the Mayfair is lovely. Good morning countryside? I look out on great sycamores and the quiet of Grosvenor Square. Little would one know that I am in the heart of England's capital and one of the poshest parts of London. At the Millennium Mayfair, room service is delivered on its highest level. White clothed table complete with flower in vase. It could make one want to stay forever or say, 'I do.' As I did when my now husband proposed to me over an elegant breakfast here. It feels like home.

"Also extraordinary and friendly is the Millennium Mayfair's concierge, Nic Lander. He's an exceptional human being who goes above and beyond expectations with joy. I'll never forget my first stay at the Millennium Mayfair. I had recently finished a show in New York where I played a journalist from the 1980s. The costume required me to wear fake Lee press-on nails for the run of the show. Once the show closed, my nails were so weak from this bit of costume that shortly after, while in London, a nail ripped straight through the center, making it difficult to use the hand. On a Sunday, Nic Lander somehow had nail glue show up at my hotel room door!

"One jewel inside the Mayfair is Akasa, the Millennium Mayfair's fine dining restaurant. It's a peaceful atmosphere that welcomes guests and the community. You can watch the friendly chef prepare your dinner or rather, delicious works of art, right before your eyes and admire the care and creativity he puts into them first hand! His dishes are designed artistically on the plate and the taste matches the high artistry. I had the bolognaise as a main course, which I would absolutely go back for!"

—Katherine Boynton

As a sidekick to Nic Lander is the large charity teddy bear that makes a warm impression as guests walk into the lobby. It reflects the compassionate treatment one will receive while staying at the London Millennium Mayfair Hotel.

The "Ask Alfred" children's concierge is available as an add-on amenity to any room package. It includes the exclusive Ask Alfred cuddly teddy bear for keeps, twelve Ask Alfred color-me collectible postcards, Surf Sweets (the country's leading organic and non-chocolate chewy candy brand specializing in gummy candies and jellybeans), and an Ask Alfred cinch backpack. When a family buys this package, Millennium Hotels and Resorts will make a donation to the Dream Factory which grants the dreams of critically and chronically ill children. Ninety percent of the funds raised by the Dream Factory are used to grant dreams. There is also a £12 Little Bear Afternoon Tea for the younger set that includes an Ask Alfred teddy bear to take home.

In its own refined and understated way, the Millennium Hotel London Mayfair is on par with the very best hotels in London, including Claridge's and The London Ritz. Of course, it lacks the gilded physicality of The Ritz, the incredible tradition and savoir faire of Claridge's. But it has that most important commodity: "location, location, location." The Times real estate benchmark, and indeed its location in Mayfair on Grosvenor Square near Hyde Park and the elegant Park Lane, give it a cozy lived-in feeling, especially for longer-stay guests, that's hard to imagine at The Ritz or The Savoy.

The Millennium Mayfair is part of the worldwide empire of one of the greatest hoteliers in the world. That man is Chairman Kwek, Kwek Leng Beng of the Hong Leong Group and the Millennium & Copthorne Hotels plc worldwide. He's the boss. But he's not only the boss. His personal tastes are reflected in his hotels. He has a great knack for real estate. That's part of the equation, certainly. But he also had a knack for presentation — and finance.

His hotels in London include The Millennium Hotel Mayfair, Bailey's (built in the 1890s), Gloucester and Knightsbridge as well as the well known 833-room Copthorne Tara Hotel located in a quiet corner of the Royal Borough of Kensington and Chelsea. Chairman Kwek loves London, its antiquity, charm, history. But he's also there to make a profit.

Wikipedia, the online encyclopedia, is as good a place as any to find the basic facts of the Chairman's background. The following is what the Wikipedia has to say about him, somewhat revised by more recent information I've obtained:

"Kwek's father, the late Kwek Hong Png left Fujian province as a penniless teenager for Singapore and subsequently founded the Hong Leong Group there. Kwek Leng Beng was trained as a lawyer in London, but chose to join the family business in the early 1960's. He became Executive Chairman in 1990 and went on to establish an international reputation for his leadership of the Hong Leong Group Singapore, a conglomerate with more than 250 companies, including eleven listed ones.

"Kwek is the Executive Chairman of City Developments Limited (CDL), an international property and hotel conglomerate and a leading real estate developer listed on the Singapore Exchange Limited. The CDL Group operates in twenty countries in Asia, Europe, North America and New Zealand/Australia and has over 300 subsidiaries and associated companies including five companies listed on the stock exchanges of London, Hong Kong, New Zealand and the Philippines. CDL has a market capitalization of over US$6 billion (at its peak, it reached over US$10 billion) and is in the top 5 percent of listed companies in Singapore. It is also the second-biggest property developer in Southeast Asia.

"Kwek Leng Beng also chairs Millennium & Copthorne (M&C) Hotels plc, which is a London-listed international hotel group of which 54 percent share belongs to CDL. M&C is ranked 34th among the world's top international hotel groups (Index of 325 World's Largest Hotel Groups, July 2009, *Hotels* magazine) and has a portfolio of over 120 hotels with over 36,000 rooms in eighteen countries.

"Kwek's Hong Leong Group of companies also owns Hong Leong Finance, Singapore's largest finance company, with a network of twenty-eight branch offices. Kwek Leng Beng was a member of the Board of Trustees of the Singapore Management University. He also holds an honorary doctorate (DUniv) from Oxford Brookes University. Kwek oversees the Singaporean operations of the Hong Leong Group while his cousin and fellow billionaire Quek Leng Chan oversees the Malaysian operations."

One can also turn to a more established source of information, Reuters, to get additional info on the prodigiously hard-working Chairman:

"Kwek Leng Beng has been the Chairman of M&C since its incorporation. He is the Executive Chairman of the Hong Leong Group Singapore and CDL. He is also Chairman and Managing Director of Hong Leong Finance Limited and City e-Solutions Limited and the Chairman of Hong Leong Asia Ltd. Mr Kwek's achievements have also captured the attention of the academic institutions. He was conferred: Honorary Doctorate of Business Administration in Hospitality from Johnson & Wales University (Rhode Island, US), where students have an opportunity to pursue career education in business, hospitality, culinary arts or technology; Honorary Doctorate from Oxford Brookes University (UK) whose citation traced how Mr. Kwek, who joined the family business in the early 1960s, had gone on to establish an international reputation for his leadership of the Hong Leong Group, as well as being an active supporter of higher education in Singapore.

"Mr. Kwek also serves as a Member of the INSEAD East Asia Council. France-based INSEAD is one of the world' leading and largest graduate business schools which bring together people, cultures and ideas from around the world. Mr. Kwek is a Member of the Action Community of Entrepreneurship (ACE), which involves both the private and public sectors to create a more entrepreneurial environment in Singapore for small and medium enterprises.

"Mr. Kwek has distinguished himself in property investment and development, hotel ownership and management, financial services and industrial enterprises. Today, he sits on the flagship of a multi-billion empire worth over US$21 billion in diversified premium assets worldwide and stocks traded on seven of the world's stock markets. He currently heads a worldwide staff strength of some 40,000 across a range of businesses in Asia-Pacific, the Middle East, Europe and North America. Mr Kwek also played a pivotal advisory role in Las Vegas Sands Corporation's successful bid for Singapore's high profile Integrated Resort project at the Marina Bay."

Even a partial account of the Chairman's career provides insight as to why he is a billionaire.

By the by, another of Chairman Kwek's great London properties is the Millennium Hotel London Knightsbridge, which counts many designer stars of today such as Gucci, Chanel and other designer boutiques as its close neighbors. Conveniently located at 17 Sloane Street, the hotel is just two minutes from the world famous Harrods Department Store and Hyde Park. Sloane Street has always been on par with Bond Street (which is five minutes away from the Millennium Mayfair). These two streets, which house many of the world's famous, top fashion brands, have long earned their reputation as London's most exclusive, chic shopping belts. Transportation is a breeze as the Knightsbridge underground tube station a just a good nine iron golf shot of 150 yards away. Its MU Restaurant and Cocktail Bar is a destination for local fashionistas with its innovative Asia-accented French cuisine.

According to ZillionTech's Knowledge Repository, Chairman Kwek used to "sit in the lobby of King's Hotel at Havelock Road in the Seventies in Singapore and pray that guests would check in. 'When they arrived, I cheered and my spirits lifted,' he recalls."

Real estate was the family business when Chairman Kwek was young. During that time, it was common for developers to enter the hospitality market as an auxiliary business. There was never any intention to start a chain of hotels, which has now become quite fashionable. That formula would change dramatically when young Kwek eventually took control of the company.

But back in 1967, Chairman Kwek's father asked him to look for a land site, to build the King's Hotel. This milestone heralded the company's venture into the hotel arena. In 1970, when his father's company opened King's Hotel in Singapore, Kwek Leng Beng was assigned the task of managing it. This sounded like it might be a dream job, hanging around a beautiful hotel all day, but it was really a sort of business baptism by fire. With little knowledge or experience in managing hotels, the young Kwek was thrown into the deep end of the pool. He was either going to swim or sink.

Meanwhile, Kwek's father was managing the smaller Orchid Inn Hotel at Dunearn Road, which had fewer rooms than King's but the father made more money with it than the son did with King's. Learning why that was so would be the young Kwek's first lesson in the hotel business.

Chairman Kwek persevered. In 1998, King's Hotel was rebranded Copthorne King's. He was rebranding several of his hotels in Singapore after having acquired the Copthorne hotel chain and integrated it into the Millennium Hotels. Name recognition is very big in hotels, and Copthorne was well known. The newly dubbed Copthorne King's also underwent extensive renovations at this same time, to the tune of $15 million (in Singapore dollars) or approximately US$10.7 million.

Over the years, King's proved to be quite the excellent training ground for the young Kwek. He learned how to navigate through economic downturns, what to do with an over-supply of hotel rooms and how to balance the waxing and waning flow of tourists to Singapore. In the process, King's blossomed from its original 175 rooms to 310 Zen-inspired rooms today. The hotel mostly caters to businessmen these days. The great thing about businessmen is that they show up at your hotel even if the weather's lousy! Not like those finicky tourists.

Chairman Kwek must have studied his new trade very hard, because today, his company owns over 120 hotels across five continents. There is still a soft spot in the Chairman's heart, however, for his first hotel, King's. Having practically raised it from a pup, and having bought the land it occupies for just under a million in Singapore bucks in 1967. Of course, today, that same property, which encompasses the land and the hotel building itself, is worth northwards of S$120 million (US$86.4 million). As the Chairman himself has explained it, "If you work backwards, this means that the investment at King's has enjoyed a 10.5 percent annual compounded rate of return, without even taking into account the good dividends received yearly on this property." Pretty good return on your Singapore dollar, yes?

In fact, Chairman Kwek firmly believes that "real estate is the key to becoming rich in this part of the world (East Asia)." Not that it won't earn you a nice living in other parts of the world. The Chairman's company also owns Los Angeles' Millennium Biltmore Hotel, where they used to throw that Oscar shindig every year before they moved it to that big ugly auditorium place. And the company also owns Chicago's Millennium Knickerbocker, where a fellow by the name of Al Capone once hung out in the Twenties.

But Copthorne King's will always be home for the Chairman. He affectionately calls King's "the mother of all hotels." Rightfully so. After all, this is where he started as a rookie. This is where he learned the ropes of the business. Much sweat (literally) and perseverance went into building the hotel and, sentimentally, it was also the family's first hotel investment. He returns to it every chance his busy international schedule permits, and when he's in town, he's sure to visit it weekly. He likes to dine there with family members, business associates and tennis buddies. You can most often find him at the hotel's famous long Penang Peranakan buffet table. The Chairman is partial to the *Penang Hokkien mee*. He also likes the King's Tient Court restaurant. Well, if you worked as hard as the Chairman, you'd have a pretty good appetite too.

We have stayed at the Millennium Mayfair several times, actually three in all, and these stays were progressively better. During one mem-orable stay, our suite had a large bedroom, a mid-sized living room, and two bathrooms. I had an especially long stay, about a week, in 2007 when I interviewed Chairman Kwek. The consummate host, I met Chairman Kwek for dinner at the L'Atelier de Joël Robuchon Restau-rant, steps from the bright lights of Piccadilly Circus. I understand from the Chairman that he has plans to revamp the Mayfair and make it a flagship establishment for M&C Hotels plc.

"I will tell you why we have more hotels here than in New York," he said. "The gross operating profit — margin — in Lon-don is better than in New York."

"Does the high cost of operating in New York — the unions and . . . ?" I asked.

"Yes, the hotel industry has no unions in the UK."

"I refused a sale on the UN Plaza," he went on. It's a little difficult to keep the Chairman focused on one nation's hotels at a time. He tends to think globally. Here he's referring to an offer for his UN Plaza Hotel in Manhattan that, apparently, he could refuse. "I didn't need the money and New York has always been a great city for hotels . . . There is only one UN. How many ho-tels around the world can call themselves the UN Plaza?"

In fact, it's a little hard for anyone to keep track of all the hotels the Chairman manages, or owns, or both. A colleague of his told me, "In the absolute number of hotels that they (Copthorne) actually own, rather than help people to manage, I think Chairman Kwek is the leader. They own over 120 hotels around the world, and I don't think there is any individual or company that owns that many hotels. Others may manage many, many, more." That's the real estate mogul in the Chairman. He just has this thing for acquiring property that he inherited from his pop. When you or I find a hotel we like in a beautiful location, we book a room. The Chairman buys the place.

"We created the first hospitality REIT [real estate investment trust] in Singapore and it has been performing very well," the Chairman continued. "In the first eighteen months after its listing, the share price had already gone up by 300 percent." Today, after the financial crisis and the rebound in the stock market, the share price has increased about 100 percent against its initial listing price.

"Is it still a good investment — Singapore?" I asked.

"Singapore just released a projection on Friday, and growth will be four to six percent against last year of eight to nine percent." (This was said in the context before the 2007/08 global meltdown.)

Chairman Kwek is also developing hotels in India — business class price without the grand ballroom and conference centers. "When this budget hotel is developed and its earnings are stabilized, we hope to achieve about US$150 per room," he said.

His hotel in Paris is The Millennium Hotel Paris Opéra. I stayed there just before my book on his Broadway Hudson Theater was published. I was astonished to find myself sitting in the rounded living room in the hotel, looking out at the busy Boulevard Haussman and the pinnacle of the Paris Opera House. Part of me can sense the Germans approaching Paris in the famous movie *Casablanca*; another part of me: Hemingway's *A Moveable Feast*, his views of Paris as the epitome of literature, music, art and just plain life.

Here after writing *Life at the Top: Inside New York's Grand Hotels* I'm planning another book about hotels, but can't help but marvel at Chairman Kwek's far-flung hotel empire, at once modern and sleek, and alternately historic, grand, brimming with the best of the past and blending this with the best of the present and future.

As I indicated, the Millennium Mayfair is one of many hotels Millennium he owns in London. Bailey's is a traditional hotel, and historic, another of the Chairman's London properties. Built in the 1890s, it's right next to the Gloucester Hotel in Kensington, which is, surprise surprise, also a Millennium Hotel.

34

I got another rare opportunity to sit and chat with Chairman Kwek one late fall afternoon in 2008, in the posh restaurant of his Millennium Knightsbridge Hotel in the heart of London's fashionable shopping — Sloane Street. Our talk ranged from Gucci, Fendi and other designer shops that line the fabled street, to the hotel across the water in New York City, to the Hudson Theatre.

"This hotel, it was a Holiday Inn long time ago," he said, referring to the hotel we were in at the moment, as we tasted a special noodle dish. "They had a swimming pool on this level, and then somebody from South Africa took it over. Then during the recession, American Express offered me this deal. And I fully refurbished the hotel."

In 1995, his Hong Kong-listed CDL Hotels International acquired the Copthorne group with hotels in the UK, France and Germany. The Copthorne hotels, his London hotels and other hotels were pooled together into the Millennium and Copthorne (M&C) Hotels plc and floated on the London Stock Exchange in 1996. M&C took over the business undertakings and hotel assets under CDL Hotels International. Both Copthorne and Millennium brands have been growing since.

Along with the Knightsbridge Hotel in which my conversation took place, Chairman Kwek owns the Millennium Gloucester and the Millennium Bailey's Hotel in London. The Chairman once took Steve Wynn to the Bombay Brasserie, an Indian restaurant which has made a name for itself as a favorite of celebrities, at Millennium Bailey's. "Was he considering becoming a partner?" I asked. "No, no. He was here, at that time, when London was supposed to be — England was supposed to be — opening up to international casino operators and owners, so he was looking at London, and I happened to be here. I've known him a year. So we talked and I took him to see the Bailey's Hotel. He liked the Bombay Brasserie which he said he could envision a similar concept to be placed in one of his establishments in Las Vegas."

Chairman Kwek spends two-thirds of each year in Singapore where his Hong Leong Group is headquartered and where he was born and raised. The other third of the time he spends playing an active role in the asset management of his vast hotel and other holdings around the globe. He views himself as a real estate developer first, a hotelier second, learning much about real estate from his late father.

"My father came from China originally," he said. "He started as a building materials supplier and he went into real estate, not as a developer at first. His first love was real estate. I took over the chairmanship of Hong Leong Group in 1990, although I had been actively leading several companies within the group before that."

The Chairman, ever practical, talked about his group of hotels, including the historical Biltmore Los Angeles where the Academy Awards ceremonies were once held, after they were first at The Roosevelt. "I'm not trying to build a huge hotel chain like Starwood or Intercontinental. I just can't do that as I don't have critical mass. But I, unlike the purely hotel-trained people, have real estate experience. M&C has consistently adopted a twin strategy of being both an owner and operator of hotels. For instance, with the Biltmore Hotel, I see the potential of maximizing the plot ratio and I plan to convert, at the right time, some of the offices within the Biltmore, and hope to re-configure some two hundred rooms into condominiums."

Chairman Kwek explained he was a real maverick in the hotel business. "I'm a contrarian in the sense that many hotel companies want to get all the management contracts they can, around the world. My approach to hotels is not only management but also owning the real estate. I have an extra strategy. With many of my hotels like the Biltmore, we can eventually convert a significant part, if not, the entire site (where it makes business sense) into condominiums or other uses. I've also introduced branded residences into Singapore by developing the St. Regis Hotel in Singapore, which has adjoining St. Regis Residences where residents are able to tap the hotel services. Today, The St. Regis Hotel Singapore is one of the world's best luxury hotels."

Since its grand opening in April 2008, The St. Regis Singapore has earned prestigious accolades and been named one of the best new hotels by renowned publications, including *Condé Nast Traveller* Hot List

2008, *Travel + Leisure* IT list 2008, Robb Report Best of the Best List 2008, and *Elite Traveller's* 101 Top Suites in the World.

I was still ruminating on how the Chairman's hotels are, for him, also real estate. "The hotels have another life," I said.

"They have another life," he said. "So what we want to do now is to seriously look at some of our hotels, to reposition them, bringing some of the hotels to a much higher standard. In fact I have a designer doing a prototype design of the rooms for me in Singapore. The design is 'East Meets West.' It's a fusion between East and West because I strongly believe that, you know, Chinese travel will become the dominant traveling force in years to come. In four or five years, they will be the greatest travelers. And I want them to feel that they are at home when they travel. It's not exactly Asian design. It's the luxury of the West, and a touch of the East."

In fact, a number of rooms at the Millennium Biltmore have been designed this way. "The Biltmore, which currently has about 683 rooms, could have been converted into an 850 room hotel, I think" he said.

"The previous owner of the Biltmore left two floors empty with structures that could be partitioned and made into additional hotels rooms. We have plans to convert one of the office blocks into residences at the appropriate time. Because downtown Los Angeles is getting very popular. People living in L.A. have found that they have to drive for two to three hours every morning, be stuck in traffic jams before they can come downtown. So the condominium prices there are very good now. And it is fashionable to have condominiums inside the hotel providing the hotel services to the condominiums."

These were plans that were shared when the market outlook was brighter in 2006. Although the plans were already drawn up, in light of the global financial meltdown in 2007/08, this redevelopment initiative was put on hold as it was deemed unsustainable given the challenging economic conditions. Perhaps, one day, at the right time, when the economy stabilizes and there is growth, they may revisit this idea.

I admitted to the Chairman that I was curious about his own lodging preferences.

"When in London, sometimes I stay in my hotel, sometimes I stay in my apartment," the Chairman explained. "In fact," he said, "when you have a chance, there is another historic hotel called Millennium Hotel Paris Opéra, located in the heart of the business area, close to the major stores of the Faubourg Saint-Honoré and the Place Vendôme and to the main monuments. It's a small hotel, only 167 rooms, it's not far from the Grand Opera House. But uniquely (and not many know this), when you stand in front of the hotel, facing it, from the side view of the hotel, you get a beautiful vista of Sacré-Coeur Basilica up high on Montmartre."

Later, the Chairman drove me to his Bailey's Hotel and the Glouces-ter Hotel, both in Kensington, in his Rolls-Royce. I assumed he would have a chauffeur. When I got into the back seat, he motioned me to sit in the front seat because he was driving.

Getting back to the Millennium Mayfair, a number of the houses around Grosvenor Square date back before the American Revolution-ary War. Much more commercial than residential these days, Grosvenor Square, like nearby Berkeley Square, was one of London's most fash-ionable residential addresses until WWII. But before and after the war, the private houses were razed, replaced by hotels, embassies, and neo-Georgian apartment flats.

I have a special affection for Grosvenor Square as I stayed in a suite with my son and his mother when I first interviewed Kwek Leng Beng. A number of years later, I proposed to my soul mate Katherine. Our suite overlooked the park and I took special comfort from the statue of American President Franklin Delano Roosevelt.

Former U.S. presidential candidate Adlai E. Stevenson died outside after leaving the American Embassy. His companion Marietta Tree says his last words were, "Do not walk so fast . . . and do hold your head up, Marietta."

The homes around Grosvenor Square were where "the Bentley Boys," English versions of F. Scott Fitzgerald's idle, rich and playful American counterparts and ex-patriots, held all-day parties. I had thought they were the owners of the Bentley Motor Car showrooms on Berkeley Square. But their name came from their predilection for green Bentley sports cars. Some of their names seemed to fit their reputation — especially "Woolf" Barvato; the others were Tim Birkin, Glen Kidston and Bernard Rubin.

In March, 2009, I had dinner at the Millennium Mayfair Hotel's Shogun restaurant in the charming company of that indefatigable London hotel PR executive, Julia Record. In 2014 Katherine and I had dinner there with Chairman Kwek himself. The Shogun is a highly lauded Japanese restaurant offering a full range of deliciously exotic fare to suit just about any palate. The earth-toned room is the coziest "dungeon" you've ever seen, with racks of feathered arrows, Japanese watercolors, and other intriguing period touches decorating it. Chairman Kwek touts it as the most authentic and best sushi and sashimi restaurant. It's certainly the one he enjoys most.

Just over 400 years earlier Guy (also known as Guido) Fawkes was imprisoned in the former underground Mayfair prison now housing the restaurant. Guy Fawkes Day is celebrated on November 5, on the anniversary of his attempt to blow up the Houses of Parliament in protest to systematic discrimination against English Roman Catholics. We had a more enjoyable experience than Mr. Fawkes, I suspect, as we were treated to an unforgettable quadruple course sushi and other appetizing entries there for dinner.

Next to Bailey's is the Millennium Gloucester with over 600 guest rooms. A convention hotel in every way, with every size meeting space, one of them is roomy enough to oblige automobiles. The guest rooms have direct dial telephone, trouser press, Guestlink TV, in-room movies and satellite, coffee and tea making facilities, en suite bathroom and hairdryer. Guests staying in the Millennium Club Rooms have access to a private Millennium Club Lounge where they can enjoy complimentary breakfasts, evening cocktails and coffee throughout the day. South West 7 has Italian cuisine in a rich, warm ambiance. Bugis Street Brasserie serves authentic Singaporean Chinese food and a selection of Asian dishes. Back Page Sports Bar has a true London pub atmosphere while Humphrey's Bar is a cosmopolitan lobby bar with live music.

Originally, the hotel business was simply about sheltering people for a night. Travelers, particularly in England, traversed the various king's roads and, since it often took days to get anywhere, the coach had to put up someplace at night. Eventually, however, a different tradition began to take hold in the best of London's hotels. And that was the tradition of gentlemanly "service." It's not really surprising in a country famous for not only its nobility but for its butlers, that the British would have a particularly good knack for making people feel right at home.

Millennium Bailey's Hotel Exterior

Bailey's Bar

Bailey's Olives Restaurant

Bailey's King Size Room

Chelsea Harbour Exterior Veiw

Chelsea Harbour Abingdon Suite

Chelsea Harbour Riverside Brasserie

Chelsea Harbour Pool and Spa

Ham Yard Drawing Room

Ham Yard Courtyard View

A Ham Yard Suite

Another Ham Yard Suite

Millennium Mayfair Hotel Exterior

Millennium Mayfair Lobby

Millennium Mayfair Ballroom

Millennium Mayfair Luxury Suite

THE LANESBOROUGH

As we mentioned earlier we have come to the conclusion that London's greatest grand hotels really reflect the vision and creativity of their managers and owners just as much if not more than the budgets of the companies which own and run them. I've seen this time and time again. To separate The Lanesborough from its managing director, fourth generation hotelier Geoffrey Gelardi, is impossible. His grandfather was managing director of the Waldorf Towers in New York at a time when The Waldorf-Astoria and its highest floors called the Waldorf Towers were considered the greatest hotel in the world. Gelardi, who launched the Lanesborough in 1991 and oversaw its renovation by the late interior designer Alberto Pinto, had already spent twenty years with world renowned hotels. The Lanesborough, now part of the Oetker Collection, sits opposite Appley House, once the home of the Duke of Wellington. Reportedly the most expensive hotel in London, this is really saying something as London is one of the most expensive cities in the world.

> "It's a business where you are not paid very much in the early stage and you have to work quite hard, but it never bothered me," Gelardi told *Luxury Travel Advisor Magazine*. "I enjoyed my work so much I didn't care if they paid me or not."

When considering an offer to open The Lanesborough, Gelardi visited the major competition and according to the interview in *Luxury Travel Advisor* he found that "the service was not friendly; it was too English. In opening the Lanesborough, we wanted a quintessentially

English hotel but without the pompous British attitude." Along with relaxing the dress code for guests and making sure the hotel was up to the high-tech standard of the times, he provided butlers for every room and suite, and he himself sat through butler classes to learn how butlers should act.

My son Will Morehouse has singularly fond memories of staying at the hotel.

Frank Marrenbach, CEO of the Oetker Collection, noted, "The Lanesborough is clearly a landmark within the European hospitality landscape with an exceptional heritage and a strong and unique identity, fitting perfectly in our Collection of Masterpiece Hotels."

The hotel was recreated by the world renowned Alberto Pinto Studio, visionary designers of grand interiors. The Regency style that has been a special part of The Lanesborough's history has been carefully maintained, adding the latest in modern luxuries for the discerning traveler. After an extensive renovation, the hotel reopened in the spring of 2015 with ninety-three fresh rooms and suites and elegant dining.

"Oetker Collection is one of the most inspiring selections of masterpiece hotels in the world," according to the Oetker Collection website. "The name 'masterpiece hotels' includes a pledge: a commitment to provide service of the highest quality, every hour of every day. The pearl as a symbol [Oetker's logo is a circle of pearls] combines singularity, beauty and quality. The individual pearls bind together to form a unique string of pearls.

"Each property is one-of-a-kind, reflecting the unique European heritage and sharing the highest levels of service internationally with exceptional and historical architecture and interiors combining with great attention to detail.

"The renovation honors the building's architectural heritage as one of London's most revered Regency landmarks. It embodies the signature style that has become synonymous with The Lanesborough, while incorporating the latest in contemporary luxury and technological innovations."

Other Properties in the Oetker Collection

L'Apogée Courchevel — a luxury chalet with a warm and family atmosphere offering the most desirable skiing experience at the top of Courchevel 1850 in the French Alps.

Brenners Park-Hotel & Spa — an iconic grand hotel, amidst a sprawling private park in Baden-Baden, Germany. The historic Villa Stéphanie now offers Europe's most refined and innovative spa experience.

Le Bristol Paris — an authentic vibrant French palace completely refurbished, the ultimate reference for Parisian art-de-vivre, ideally located on the prestigious rue du Faubourg Saint-Honoré.

Château Saint-Martin & Spa — a romantic chateau of excellence nestled in the heart of Provence, boasting breathtaking views over the Mediterranean coastline.

Eden Rock — a luxurious retreat in St. Barths built on a rocky promontory, surrounded by white sandy beaches and turquoise sea; French art-de-vivre in the heart of the Caribbean.

Fregate Island Private — a jewel of conservation featuring lush forest, wild fauna, and overlooking the crystal waters of the Seychelles. Unique on the planet.

Hotel du Cap-Eden-Roc — a legendary luxury hotel at the centre of a scenic private park, where old-world glamour meets modern luxury at the top of the Cap d'Antibes.

Palais Namaskar — a peaceful oasis with contemporary and sophisticated design set in the Palmeraie, the most exclusive residential area in Marrakech.

THE CHELSEA HARBOUR HOTEL

"Boats bob in the gentle harbor. A panoramic view of the Thames River and the great Ferris wheel called 'The Eye' is what I see in the moonlight from my balcony at The Chelsea Harbour Hotel. I breathe in cool October air. It's quiet and refreshing. Although geographically located in 'downtown' London, here I feel an escape. A privacy. Spacious modern suites have all comforts including five-star room service and separate sleeping and living areas. We dinned in at the Chelsea Riverside Brasserie. It was a peaceful and relaxing evening, especially with the lovely marina view from our table."

—Katherine Boynton

Situated in one of London's most exclusive areas, in a stunning location overlooking Chelsea Harbour Marina and the River Thames, The Chelsea Harbour Hotel is a tranquil waterfront oasis and London's only five-star, all-suite hotel. And where else in London, the cultural capitol of the world, do you have a fleet of pleasure cruises and speed boats right out your window?

Enjoy breathtaking views over London from the hotel's penthouse level in the Albert and Battersea suites. These suites can be combined to form a single space that can seat up to eighty people. When using these suites, the adjoining Executive Lounge is available for guests to relax and entertain in.

The Drakes suite boasts floor to ceiling windows, offering spectacular marina views, and can accommodate up to 140 guests for a dinner dance. The suite has a private terrace where guests can enjoy the fresh air and views across Chelsea Harbour.

"Our experienced team is on hand to ensure your event is truly special," a hotel brochure says. "Our chefs have designed delectable menus and we can customize them to meet your requirements and suit your tastes. Beyond meeting agendas, we offer a wealth of options to recharge; your guests can rejuvenate in our spa, or with a sightseeing tour, individually tailored to your interests by our expert concierge team."

Visit Chelsea Riverside Brasserie for breakfast, lunch or dinner. Let their talented chefs tempt your senses with delicious international dishes, using only the finest ingredients.

At The Harbour Bar, you can enjoy a wide variety of refreshments, including all day dining and afternoon tea, and in the evening, soak up the majestic views of Chelsea Harbour Marina while sipping a refreshing cocktail on the terrace.

Each of the 154 elegant one-bedroom suites, many of which have a sofa bed and connecting options, has been thoughtfully laid out and offers guests luxurious and contemporary amenities, as well as complete privacy. Additionally, experience a touch of exclusivity with four spectacular penthouse suites, situated on the top floor of the hotel. Each one has been individually designed around a unique theme, and they offer some of the best panoramic views in London from their spacious roof terraces. It's like having a townhouse in the sky with river views!

HOTEL CAFÉ ROYAL

And at my feet the pale green Thames
Lies like a rod of rippled jade.
                    —Oscar Wilde (*Symphony in Yellow*)

"The Hotel Café Royal is Oscar Wilde and Oscar Wilde is the Hotel Café Royal. For me, a special touch was the poem left on my pillow before bed, Oscar Wilde's *Symphony in Yellow*. You will have sweet dreams after reading Wilde's poetic painting of London in autumn.

Modern cutting-edge elegance with a warm touch is reflected in the décor and staff. Here you'll walk down warm oak hallways speckled with purple orchids that create a peaceful journey to your suite. Everything works smoothly with the press of a button and the comfort is heavenly. The Hotel Café Royal is conveniently located in the heart of Piccadilly Circus and steps to The West End and theater land. While here, one can honor the great history of Oscar Wilde in the gilded Grill Room, which he actually frequented. Or, for a more modern and chic experience, sip a coffee and have a pastry at Le Café with big glass windows, letting in great light and looking onto Regent Street. Your favorite part may be the Grand Hotel's five star luxurious spa and pool, or the Ten Room, a fine dining restaurant where I had the Lobster "Pompadour," truly fit for royalty. Thank you, Café Royal, for embracing the best of the old and new worlds."

—Katherine Boynton

The Café Royal wears boxing as well as literary and music (rock) hats. Celebrities such as Louis Armstrong and Muhammad Ali were all part of "The Café" routine.

In 1973 David Bowie famously retired his alter ego, Ziggy Stardust, with a star-studded party dubbed "The Last Supper." Guests included the biggest rock stars of the time such as Mick Jagger, Lou Reed and many others.

In 1951 Café Royal became the home of the National Sporting Club, holding black tie dinners before bouts often frequented by Muhammad Ali. The original National Sporting Club founders, the Earl of Lonsdale and the fifth Marquis of Queensberry, also laid down their set of boxing rules, "The Queensberry Rules for Boxing," here in 1867.

As the spiritual home of boxing and as a nod to this profound heritage, the Akasha Holistic Wellbeing Centre offers one-to-one boxing with Marianne "Golden Girl" Marston — professional fighter, protégé of Smokin' Joe Frazier, and Akasha's instructor.

With over forty years of experience at the helm of this and other top hotels, Anthony Lee was appointed General Manager of Hotel Café Royal in January 2014. While he has since left the property he remains a London hotel legend.

Anthony began his career at The Connaught Hotel and was the General Manager of this prestigious property from 2000 to 2010. Under his leadership, he steered the hotel through three different ownerships from Savoy Group to Blackstone and latterly Quinlan's private ownership. For three years prior to his stellar stint at the Cafe Royal, Anthony was General Manager of the Mayfair Hotel.

Of his appointment to Café Royal hotel, Mr. Lee commented, "I am thrilled to be joining such a wonderful team in an iconic place that will rightly take its place on the world stage. I am looking forward to working with the team to take Hotel Café Royal to the next level."

Georgi Akirov, Founder and Chairman of The Set Hotels, said, "Anthony is renowned for his grounded management style, ensuring attention to detail, and delivering an exceptionally high standard of service to his guests. We are very happy that he is joining the Hotel Café Royal family."

Anthony Lee says, "So, many layers that have gone into the thinking of design and technology. To keep it simple comes out in a way that when you ask a guest, 'how was your stay?' the answer is 'it was lovely.'

"What is it that made it lovely? It was all these hundreds of little layers that go into making it just a lovely experience.

"We have little sound sensors ... we know there's human life in the room. We don't know who, how many, or what you're up to. We don't want to know. But we know not to knock on the door even if you forget to put the 'do not disturb' sign on the door. Like the old Far East matchsticks trick outside the door which some of us remember."

Anthony Lee rose to what many called the top of the London hotel market becoming General Manager of the prestigious Connaught in 2000. That's where I first met him in the mid 2000s and I've come to know him over the years as what I affectionately call "the Ralph Lauren of hotel managers" in a market — London — that is second to none. He knits a hotel staff together like an expertly, expensively tailored Ralph Lauren cashmere sports coat. Katherine agreed as we all met over afternoon coffee in Le Café during our most recent trip:

> "It was an absolute pleasure to meet Anthony Lee. He's refined, radiates respect, consideration and accuracy. I liked him immediately. During our meeting he graciously reminded me it was almost 5:00 PM, time for my appointment to see their spa. He made me feel comfortable."
>
> —Katherine Boynton

In fact, one of Mr. Lee's loyal clients at The Connaught was Lauren himself, who thought so much of the staircase at the Connaught he had a duplicate made for his New York flagship store.

Granted the Hotel Café Royal had a lot to build on as the original Café Royal was frequented by such luminaries as H. G. Wells, Virginia Woolf, Noël Coward, and Winston Churchill.

Anthony Lee Commented:

"It's fine tuning that without (the guests) realizing it is behind the scenes. There has to be a natural interaction between the hotel and its guests …"

"For example breakfast in the morning is one of those meal periods where it's either right or wrong. It's Russian roulette, and it's not pre-booked so you can suddenly get hammered …"

"On point, it's the way you approach guests. For instance, when you say, 'What would you like to drink?'

Guest: 'I'd like English breakfast tea.'

'Right,' says the waiter. 'I'd better put the kettle on!'

"It was that natural comment from the heart for that man — that genuine English humor was right. But, then again, you've got the very serious businessman who's got a lot on his mind. So it's assessing the temperature of every single guest and thinking to himself that same guest is not necessarily going to want the same thing."

"All the money in the world will buy you the most incredible building to do what you want to it. But if you want to breath life into it, it takes three things … the building, the guests, and the most important ingredient of all — the staff. I'm going to put the three together and I'm going to bake you the most unbelievable cake you've ever tasted."

"When I saw that building, I fell in love."

"I wanted them to be aware that with my thirty-one years at The Connaught, I hadn't lost my business brains."

"I had nothing to do with the design but in terms of warming it up, or pushing to warm it up, yes."

"… the 'Tea Room' — you wouldn't recognize it five months ago 'til now. We've changed it; we've warmed it up."

"Supposedly, in 1944 they came into the Oscar Wilde Bar to tell Churchill he was Prime Minister. We've changed the name of the Oscar Wilde Bar to the Wilde Bar."

"The building is here since 1865. So my challenge is that we've only been a hotel since 2012. And I need the world to know and that's a challenge."

"Max Weitzenhoffer, theatre owner and producer, I'd love

to see him here. He would relate to many of the things I've just said to you."

"We have butlers for all the rooms if you want that. We have it. In fact, The Connaught is one of the only other places that has butlers for all the rooms."

"The private members club has eight different kinds of slippers in all sizes. And every time you stay, you get to wear your customized slippers."

Combining architectural heritage with contemporary design, Hotel Café Royal features 160 rooms and suites (including six historic suites), an array of bars and restaurants, as well as high-tech meeting and event spaces. Guests can also unwind in the Akasha Holistic Wellbeing Centre.

Hotel Café Royal is the second member of The Set, a collection created to redefine the concept of the luxury hotel for sophisticated, design-literate travelers in the 21st century.

Working to an uncompromising belief that called for hotels that were not only of the moment but that would define their times and locations, architects and designers of the caliber of Piero Lissoni, David Chipperfield and Jean-Michel Wilmotte were recruited by the Akirovs to deftly rework the DNA of the grand hotel and create spaces that are contemporary in conception, whilst simultaneously evocative of the style and glamour of the past.

The Set is currently comprised of: Hotel Café Royal, London; Conservatorium Hotel, Amsterdam; and Hotel Lutetia, Paris (reopening soon after a 3-year renovation). As of this writing, Anthony Lee has moved on. Thomas Kochs has been appointed Managing Director according to eHotelier.

Thomas held the position of General Manager of Claridge's, part of Maybourne Hotel Group, for five years during which time he continued to build upon the hotel's heritage, developing and refining the hotels' restaurant and bars including the acclaimed partnership with Chef Simon Rogan to bring 'Fera' to Claridge's.

Thomas' career with Maybourne Hotel Group spans fifteen years during which time he has held hotel management positions in two of the company's properties including the relaunch and opening of the Connaught.

The old and the new are notoriously difficult to blend successfully yet The Set creates a beauty out of tension, and strives to have the best of both worlds where heritage meets contemporaneity. They are inspired by the artistic and imaginative heritage of their Grand Dame buildings and their iconic cultural city center locations.

Thomas Kochs says "I am excited to be joining the team at Café Royal, one of the most beautiful buildings in London with fascinating heritage and history to work with. Café Royal is already 'London's Living Room', a place for minds to come together and creativity to flourish, where guests can connect to and enjoy the hotel's offering. Café Royal as a hotel is three years young and at this point is clearly ready to take the next step in its journey. There are exciting things to come, which I am thrilled to be a part of".

Georgi Akirov, Chairman of The Set remarks "We are delighted and enthused for this latest appointment to our senior team at The Set hotels. We look forward to working with Thomas to continue our journey towards achieving our vision of creating stimulating and 'beautifully composed' experiences for our guests".

As we've noted elsewhere luxury isn't limited to gilded ceilings, heated walls, and triple-glassed windows, although Hotel Café Royal has all of these and more. It is a kind of spiritual place, first and foremost, where miracles of service are the norm. A friend of mine, Carol Dean, runs the film industry leader, "From the Heart Productions." "Expect a miracle" is Carol's motto. Let me put it another way for the Hotel Café Royal: it is a miracle.

HAM YARD HOTEL

The next morning the friendly doorman literally pushed the dolly from the Hotel Café Royal around the corner down the street to the Ham Yard, tucked away on a quiet street ... this element of fun continued when entering, thanks to Kit Kemp's playful and colorful sense of interior design. Visitors may wonder if they're in a museum or a hotel, though either way it's a welcoming experience. Your imagination of what's possible at a hotel will expand here.

Leaving Café Royal was unlike leaving any hotel we've ever stayed at. We went by "luggage rack." Yes, luggage rack. Not actually on it, but following close behind the doorman to the front entrance of the Ham Yard Hotel. In some ways, but not all, it was like going from cherished history to the newest and trendiest of the new.

In addition to the theater, there's an original 1950s-style bowling alley imported from Texas, Firmdale's first soholistic spa with a fully equipped gym, and the most welcoming library and drawing room I've ever seen, with handpicked books to inspire and entertain. The book collection includes a large section on London: its history, culture, and politics. The drawing room faces the leafy tree-lined courtyard and contains a large French fireplace giving the room a warm and welcoming feeling. Its walls are Kit's design covered with Christopher Farr fabric.

The Ham Yard Hotel is Firmdale's eighth London hotel. It opened on June 1, 2014. It's set in a three-quarter-acre site in Soho a few blocks from Mayfair. Tim and Kit Kemp, who own Firmdale Hotels, designed the Ham Yard with a distinctly urban village feel. Alongside the hotel's ninety-one bedrooms and suites are twenty-four residential apartments and thirteen individual stores.

Kit Kemp comments, "I saw driftwood crocodiles, now hanging on the discothèque wall downstairs, and I knew we had to find somewhere to use them. They were completely bonkers but perfect because many years ago, I used to go to a place called the Croc so I thought, 'Fantastic, we're going to create a new Croc bar.' That was one of those moments when an idea really comes together."

As with all of the Kemp's hotels, there's a handcrafted custom design feel to the interiors of the Ham Yard — unique ribbed glass and alabaster chandeliers, both custom made in India, in the restaurant, library and some bedrooms.

The Kemps commissioned a large sculpture in bronze called "Group" by Tony Cragg for the courtyard by the entrance to the hotel. "Cragg is the ultimate Renaissance man. He's an artist, engineer, teacher, and innovator. We hope that long after we've gone, Tony's sculpture will still be here," comments Kit.

Upstairs in the Ham Yard bedrooms, large, elegant headboards in bright, exciting prints provide a great contrast to beds fit with crisp, white linens. Walls are fabric covered to create another layer of warmth. "I always try to make it comfortable to watch the television from the bed or a comfortable chair," Kit says.

Travel Weekly interviewed Kit Kemp after New York's Crosby Street Hotel opened in 2009. Kit was asked why the occupancy rates were so high for the Crosby Street Hotel. "We really didn't see another hotel where all the rooms had been individually designed and with the attention to detail we have. Also, we use a lot of color and I find that everyone is trying to copy one another. It's all starting to look formulaic whereas our formula, if we have one, is to make every building look individual." She was also asked if her hotel design ideas come from fashion. She said, "I'm never off duty. I always look for inspiration wherever I go; private homes, museums, and art galleries inspire me more than other hotels."

Progressive minded people will find this hotel invigorating and fun! It's thought provoking, and the way Kit's arranged colors brings a vitality to one's soul. One surprise is the mannequin found in every room, which is a trademark. Along with your regular bar treats, you may smile as you see lace panties are an option to open. Nothing is standard; everything has artistry! From Kit Kemp's soap and shampoo line to her tea cups' design of mythical creatures in bright pink and green. The energy expressed in flower arrangements, lights, folk art, colored books in shelves, and British artists that are fortunate enough to be on display in this grand, artistic hotel, brings out the joy and imagination of one who stays here.

THE SOHO HOTEL
AND OTHER FIRMDALE HOTELS

⌦⌫

Americans in London do manage to get together! "After we did a reading of the musical *Ghost*, Alexandra Silber (a costar of a London production of *Carousel*) came by and hung out with us for a little while."

So said TV, film and theater producer David Garfinkle who is co-producing the blockbuster musical, *Spiderman, Turn Off the Dark* on Broadway, and *Ghosts* in London, and who swears by The Soho Hotel.

"I ended up eating there a lot, I was just working so hard. We stayed at The Soho Hotel on and off for a little over a week. We were doing a reading of *Ghost* so we stayed at The Soho Hotel which was just down the block from where we were rehearsing. Actually, we were divided up into a couple of hotels, but that was one of the ones . . . a lot of film and theater people stay there and the Covent Garden." Garfinkle and his fiancé, Merle Grant, a fabulous singer and dancer in her own right, are not alone in their praise of The Soho.

. . . *Liv Tyler stayed in Duplex at one of the Firmdale hotels . . . Scarlet Johansson stayed a long time at Covent Garden Hotel while doing Woody Allen's* Match Point *which also featured the hotel . . .*

I had breakfast with the elegant Angela Mannerson at The Soho. She was a public relations director for Firmdale at the time. She filled me in on the eye-catching and unique murals adorning The Soho's restaurant Refuel, and at Oscar, the restaurant of another Firmdale London hotel, Charlotte Street. "Both murals were painted by Alexander Hollweg. Refuel's features some cars, which hints at the site's previous life as a car park. Oscar's features murals painted in the style of 1916 frescoes entitled 'Scenes of Contemporary London Life' by Roger Fry and his Omega Workshop. Kit adopted this idea and commissioned Alexander Hollweg with the scenes of 21st century London as inspiration." We both cast an appreciative eye over the Refuel's mural. "It's very colorful and adds a lot of activity to the room, doesn't it?" opined Ms. Mannerson.

"On Sunday afternoons, we host the Weekend Film Club where you have a champagne afternoon tea or a three-course lunch/dinner, and then watch the movie of the week in the hotel's private screening room," she continued. "It is only £35 and such a wonderful experience because you get to obviously dine in a nice restaurant and then go and relax in a very, very comfortable screening room. The experience is very different to viewing a movie in a massive cinema, and it is also very good value for the money. Many business travelers arrive on a Sunday and they want to do something but nothing too tiring, so enjoying good food followed by a film is quite a relaxing thing to do, but constructive at the same time. It's been very popular. Films shown are ones that are at the cinema but not yet out on DVD, and it could be something like *Australia* and they've got *Slum Dog Millionaire* lined up in a couple weeks; upcoming ones would be like *The Reader*."

Each hotel has a large DVD collection at the concierge and popcorn cartons . . . Soho has more of a "pop" style or edge to it and strong media presence (being near film and media cos.); Haymarket is a John Nash building (listed) with softer interior, surrounded by theaters, hedge fund companies. etc.; Knightsbridge Hotel has old-world charm, townhouses, modern English (not "chintz"!) smaller scale but still fresh; "this hotel" contemporary London; . . . Tim and Kit like to "layer" old historic, say, fireplace, next to contemporary abstract art . . . museums using café space with better food to draw diners who then see a bit of art in the process — different kind of lure . . . licensing doesn't allow general public into Haymarket swimming pool anymore

. . . Soho has a bit of the feel like old Vermont farmhouse with wooden tables.

In some cases I have to defer to Frommer's description of London hotels: they just can't be beat. Take its descriptions of The Soho Hotel, for example: "A former parking garage in the heart of bustling Soho just became one of our favorite nests in London . . . hoteliers Kit and Tim Kemp have come up with a stunner here, a cocoon-like luxury lair in a cul-de-sac off Dean Street . . . all the famous Kemp touches can be found, from boldly striped furnishings to deep bathtubs for a late-night soak . . . the theaters of Shaftesbury and the Ivy Restaurant are only a block or two away."

Eleven hotels are featured in "Location," a booklet which describes itself as the Design Hotels Portfolio. I stayed in three of these in London including The Soho Hotel, the Metropolitan and the Haymarket Hotels. The Haymarket is located in a landmark John Nash building, next to the Haymarket Theatre. Nash helped develop a lot of Regency London. I've toured and dined in some of the other hotels including the Charlotte Street Hotel where paintings by the 20th century Bloomsbury group are juxtaposed with some fireplaces and plush chairs.

Like me and like a lot of people in the hospitality industry, "Location" is a big fan of Tim and Kit Kemp of Firmdale hotels. We've already made their acquaintance, of course, but they do seem to be all over town these days. Perhaps the secret to their success is that they own and design their every property. Their great local touch might explain why they have as yet not expanded elsewhere in the European Union, or even farther afield. On the other hand, why tamper with success? As of last check, every one of their London "boutique" hotels was booked solid.

Tim and Kit and Firmdale finally dipped their toe in the Atlantic — their first hotel outside of England opened in New York City in 2009, a gorgeous little getaway of a place called the Crosby Street Hotel. Their newest hotel, the Whitby, will be on West 56th Street just off of elegant Fifth Avenue. Finally, I have access to my London luxe life in my own backyard.

I couldn't resist contacting old acquaintance Paul Underhill, former asset manager of New York's Plaza Hotel and former President of Millennium Hotels, USA (and former London waiter!), about this potentially momentous move on the Kemps' part.

Paul said, "Probably one of the few things that becomes a challenge in New York is that in New York people expect snappier service. Lunches in England can go on! If I want to talk to you for an hour that's fine but I really want to make my order and my food to come and then I can make the decision. I think that's one challenge they (Firmdale) may have. But on the whole, good service, and friendly service, translates wherever you are in the world. The feel that you, the guest, is important. You can see that the people in the hotel, no matter how busy they are in trying to set up for the opening, are smiling at you. It doesn't matter who it is! You never know who you are talking to in a hotel. And if you get in that habit, you don't think about it, you do it automatically."

When Paul went to London to observe the quality of service at the Haymarket, The Soho and other Firmdale hotels, he came away with this: "No, I wasn't amazed. I was impressed because it is not in your face. It's not like you drive up and are greeted by five butlers! . . . Their service is rather like the decor — you grow into it. You realize that you ask someone a question and they answer it! They follow up and they get back to you!"

Of course I promptly inspected the Crosby as soon as I got back stateside. I immediately felt I was back in London. Even the cobbled street in the heart of New York's Soho art and residential neighborhood whispered London town. Each of the individually designed bedrooms and suites on eleven floors of new construction have full-length, warehouse-style windows and abundant natural light.

Of course, I put more weight on Paul's impressions than my own. Of his own visitation to the new establishment, he stressed that while the "hardware" and amenities of the hotel were of the very highest quality imaginable, the Kemps' overall emphasis is on making sure guests are comfortable. "That starts with the type of doorknobs you have," Paul explained. "The shower, all of those things — if they don't work — if an engineer knows every time he goes up to a room the door is going to fall off, he loses confidence in his product and he can't correct it. . . . But Tim (Kemp) has brought his own man over from London to paint the door numbers. The first thing that arrived in the architect's office was a door and he said, 'This is how we want the door.' There was no ifs, ands, or buts about it. And that's the kind of detail they've done with the purveyors of the drapes. All their hotels are really 'home decorated.'"

On service, Paul said, "As simple as it sounds, it isn't. It is not easy to anticipate what the client wants. That's really what it boils down to. Why is this guest standing in the lobby? Why is he worried? How can I approach that person? And it becomes an acquired sense, if you are interested in people, you come to understand . . . You can have situations where guests don't want you to go over to them!

"The thing I always say is when you're working in a hotel you're on the stage. And when you go to a restaurant you can expect people to look after you. But it's not servile to look after someone. To make someone comfortable and happy. And if you get that through members of the staff then they start to enjoy looking after people! Rather than say to themselves, 'how many more people are going to come in before I can go home!' State of mind."

Thanks, Paul. Now, back to Britannia.

The Soho is not the newest but it is the largest of these properties, and of the Firmdale empire. The others include: Charlotte Street, Covent Garden, and the Knightsbridge. (Firmdale is expanding in leaps and bounds and it's sometimes hard to keep count of their hotels; they also have the Haymarket and Number Sixteen in London.) Soho, it might be argued, is less of a boutique and more of an old-line grande dame hotel. Every room and suite in it has been decorated differently, but all reflecting some charming aspect of London life.

One might even label The Soho's rooms "large." But The Soho was built from the ground up, not converted from an earlier building. Normally, you would be hard-pressed to find property vast enough and available enough to build on in this otherwise historically dense city. Not only that, but it does seem that every other building in London has been "listed," or protected from the wrecking ball. Well, you may have wondered in the Sixties and Seventies how government officials could ever have allowed large municipalities the world over to build all those horrendously ugly, enormous parking garages. It's so that entrepreneurs like the Kemps would have something that everyone would be happy to be seen torn down so that a beautiful, trendy new hotel could go up. The Soho went up between Dean Street and Wardour Street — right in the thick of London's thriving new "medialand." But they didn't just throw up any new hotel. They somehow managed to make it look new and historic at the same time, with its classy, red-brick style and the floor-to-ceiling "warehouse-style" windows. So, happily situated in Richmond Mews, just off Dean Street, as it is, the hotel opened to near universal rave reviews in the fall of 2004. Even the youngish staff was outfitted with style, in their charcoal Mark Powell suits, lilac shirts, Paul Smith ties and John Smedley knits. Moreover, the service too seems to combine the best of the old and the new — attentive but also relaxed. In the kitchens, Robin Read's seasonal cuisine for the gorgeous Refuel restaurant and bar fits in perfectly.

Kit Kemp, as usual, must have had a ball designing the place. The lobby, for instance, sort of wanders around. Nor is anyone likely to overlook the ten-foot black Botero cat sculpture, which also puts in an appearance on the hotel's stylish stationery. But where, you ask, is the signature tailor's dummy? In this hotel it has been sculpted from clear acrylic and lit internally, and found everywhere, from the check-in desk to the guest rooms. The hotel even found inspiration in the site's former occupation, as the Alexander Hollweg mural in the Refuel Bar picks up on the old "parking-lot" theme.

The hotel offers guests two impressive lounges to choose from. The Drawing Room features impressive art amidst wide oak floorboards and French fireplaces, the whole encapsulated in hues of hot pinks and pistachio greens. If that's a little too intense for you, try the somewhat cooler library, which favors more relaxed lighting including an oddly meditative neon ladder.

Of course, the main course of any hotel is still the rooms themselves, and they do not fail to impress. The Terrace Suite is perhaps the most jaw-dropping in all of London. Not only tastefully furnished, it boasts wraparound terraces from which you can see pretty much everything in town. If your tastes, and budget, are somewhat more modest, do try the Junior Suites. And if you're planning an extended stay, look into the Apartments, which can only be described as genuine swinging London pads. Number 2, for instance, has an open-plan kitchen, large living room and master bedroom and a bathroom seemingly carved out of granite with a separate step-in shower — it's more grotto than loo. Of course there's a second bedroom suite with its own private bath. The only problem with it is that you may never want to step out the door.

Charlotte Street Hotel

Surprise, surprise, Charlotte Street Hotel is another Firmdale property which has gotten rave reviews. A five-minute walk from Oxford Street in Central London, it has much in common with the Covent Garden Hotel — the modern English look, the innovation and comfort, the emphasis on quality. Guarding the front door are two enormous gas lamps that transport you, even before you step into the hotel, back to a storied London of Dickens and Conan Doyle.

Inside the hotel isn't bad either. The pale wood floors and dados exude a certain relaxed luxury, as do the regal leather armchairs and the attractive, attentive young staff. This special feel is continued in the hotel's large open-plan bar and restaurant, named Oscar. Central London has never had it so good.

Covent Garden Hotel

Covent Garden is another creation of that mad, magical team of Tim and Kit Kemp. The dynamic duo seem to have taken over London, and absolutely no one is complaining.

As the name implies, this hotel has a fantastic location near the theater and restaurant districts, almost within shouting distance of the Royal Opera House (otherwise generally known as Covent Garden). It's also fairly near St Paul's of Covent Garden, sometimes called "the actor's church." Its Tuscan portico entrance is seen in some sets of *Pygmalion* and is where Professor Higgins meets flower girl Eliza Doolittle. Some folks later made a fairly successful stage musical of this Bernard Shaw play called *My Fair Lady.* Awww, g'wan! (what word do you mean?) No, really. It's reported that the Earl of Bedford, who was in somewhat of a financial maelstrom at the time, asked Inigo Jones, second only to Christopher Wren when it comes to London architects, to build this gem of a church — but "no better than a barn." "You shall have the best barn in London!" Jones replied.

The hotel itself couldn't be more discreet, tucked away behind its brasserie-style awnings. Inside, it gets only better, with rich wood floors and eye-catching Persian rugs. Speaking of brasseries, Brasserie Max is just off to the right as you come in, or keep going and talk to the wonderful folks at the reception desk.

The suite that I got the grand tour of was the surprisingly largish Loft Suite number 303, with lavatories up and down — the up one just off the galleried bedroom and the down one branching off from the massive entertainment room. In a hotel like this, every room is an entertainment room, really. Like everything the Kemps do, the redesigning and tinkering never end, so one can never be entirely sure what the place will look like if you stay away for any length of time. There are department store windows which change less frequently than a Kemp hotel.

If a room is more to your taste, try number 3. It's really a high-ceilinged Junior Suite with views opening onto Shaftesbury Avenue. Here, the styling is refreshing pinks and whites, pretty much everywhere. Or, try the Junior Suite number 417. It has those exposed beams which just make you feel like you're really in London, maybe downing a pint with Long John Silver. Number 417 can be quite romantic, too. It's up to you, whatever your fantasy is. Also, keep in mind the Doubles, such as number 412, which boasts a rather unusual cross-beamed ceiling. Really, nothing makes me beam like a good beam, crossed or otherwise. There's just something so storybook about them. Maybe because in the States we hardly ever see them. Mostly it's just plaster and track lighting.

The Kemp stamp has definitely been put on the bathrooms at Covent Garden, very similar to the style at the Charlotte Street Hotel, in fact. The food is auspiciously Asian but not too out-there. The Covent Garden also offers an intimate brasserie setting in its eatery. Or try the wood-paneled, impressively draped Drawing Room with its "honour" bar. Later, work it all off in the gym or the single treatment room. Or simply continue lazing around in the screening room. The hotel sponsors a weekend film club Saturday evenings that includes an attractively priced dinner-movie package.

Like all the Kemp offerings, Covent Garden Hotel is remarkable as well as comfortable. You'll generally find the clientele a tad more mature than at Charlotte Street, and its restaurant is more refined. The Firmdale hotels just seem to keep getting better and better. Who would have thought after all these decades of luxury accommodation that there would still be so much room for innovation?

Knightsbridge Hotel

One thing you have to grant London hotels — they've got the names locked up. What could be more evocative, I ask you, than Knightsbridge Hotel? The very name conjures up so many fabulous images and sensations. King Arthur seems to standing before you. Not that there's much else terribly medieval about this hotel, mind. Knightsbridge, by the way, did derive its name from the bridge that knights of the realm of yore rode over on the way in town from Windsor Castle and other remote regions.

The neighborhood of Beaufort Gardens is a generally genteel residential one. The Knightsbridge is a welcome addition to it, I think. First of all, the area needed it. Secondly, the hotel and the environs go hand-in-gauntlet. The hotel has been designed in the modern style with taste (not always the case); and the setting couldn't be more peaceful and restorative. The hotel offers most of the services a modern traveler or businessman requires these days, except for a fitness room. The rooms have been individually decorated and there are four Junior Suites, which are somewhat juxtaposed in style; one is earth tones and textures, another is startling fuchsias and slickness.

The impressive lobby houses Carol Sinclair's remarkable organic sculpture (there's that word again, "organic"), which does go peculiarly well with Peter Clark's rather fanciful collages of classic Knightsbridge dogs — mostly small breeds like Scotties and Dachshunds. After all, how relaxing would it be to lounge under a picture of a Great Dane or Irish Wolfhound?

The lobby sort of flows into the Drawing Room, which switches tones on you with its African prints. Keep going and the style switches again to a softer feel in the Library, especially Dominic Berning's clever book lights and that ladder with its rungs lit up. Of course there's an old hearth, on top of which is a John Illsley abstract. Again, the old and the new, mixed like a classic cocktail. Speaking of which, there is another "honour" bar to meet your libation requirements. The staff is another set of genuinely charming, attractive youngsters. Where do they find them? Or is it the result of some sort of crash-course, boot camp-like training school? Eton, perhaps? Rugby? No matter. The results speak for themselves, with those charming accents. The service and the house-keeping are top-notch, too.

As for specific accommodations here, I dipped my toe into number 101, which they tell me is the largest and best on hand. It certainly looked it. All the rooms, however, are "junior-style" with separate sitting areas. Their Deluxe Doubles are also impressive, I hear. I ducked into number 201 long enough to see that it looks out onto Beaufort Gardens and is furnished in a harmonious way that you couldn't have believed before you saw it with your own eyes. I also got a look at number 302, where the offering is bespoke fabric and tree-top vistas.

The suite I actually stayed in had an extensive balcony and floor-to-ceiling windows that made me happy to gaze out of and thankful I didn't have to wash them. You see, that's one of the great things about hotels. You really can enjoy your luxurious surroundings. If they were in your home, you'd be the one responsible for keeping it all so spic-and-span. It takes a hotel staff to keep house like this nowadays. The seating in my suite consisted of varnished oak and leather clad objects. And on the rare occasions when I grew tired of gazing out those Monticello-sized windows, there was satellite TV in both the sitting and bedroom areas. Further merciful amenities included excellent air-conditioning, a personal safe (into which I placed my few meager valuables if only for the sensation), a DVD player, all the outlets any nerd could want and even a cell phone provided for my use.

Snooping further about the property I could see that the bathrooms generally were of the shiny granite and oak variety, usually with twin wash basins and rather invitingly deep cast-iron tubs. I was notified that not all the baths have separate step-in showers; so you've been warned.

No doubt, unlike me, you'll be gadding all about town at night, but I was thankful for the 24-hour room service, supplying everything a midnight-fridge raider could dream of, from the homemade pizzas and hamburgers to the grilled rib-eye steaks and the Banofee Pie and Carrot Cake.

Knightsbridge Hotel has somewhat the feel of an extremely upscale B&B, but I still have very fond memories from my youthful Britrail Pass days of many a British B&B all over this lovely country at which I also felt right at home.

THE HAYMARKET HOTEL

~≈⊚ ⊚≈~

S taying at the Haymarket Hotel was idyllic several ways. First, for me, the hotel staff reminded me of "The Lambs Club" where I lived as a teenager and very young man until I got a job on the *The Christian Science Monitor* as a reporter. I had had a reporter's "tryout" on the *New York Post*, something that the Newspaper Guild benevolently set up for up-and-coming reporters. Since I had never written a news story in my life, aside from the few to qualify for a try-out, it was a grueling two months. I'd painstakingly labor on my *Post* stories as if I had been Truman Capote reworking and reworking a novella. The veteran reporters could sit down and whip something off — a half hour. I sat there in the city room it seemed for hours, finding the right word for something I had never done before.

Anyway, back to the Haymarket, which was a gentleman's club in an earlier incarnation. Before Firmdale turned it into a landmark hotel, it did serve as the headquarters for American Express. And right next to it sits a landmark theater, the Haymarket. It was here I saw a stellar *On the Waterfront* directed and starring Steven Berkoff, and it made me rejoice over what true drama could be. Starring Simon Merrells, who captured the spirit of a young Marlon Brando, who starred in the 1954 movie, I got an orchestra (or stall) seat for the incredible sum of ten pounds by getting to the box office just before curtain time. The Haymarket Theatre had opened in 1824, on July 4th of that year to be exact, with a production of Sheridan's *The Rivals*. In 1994 it had a £1.3 million refurbishment when air conditioning was also installed. The otherwise war-torn year of 1914 saw the premier performance of Ibsen's *Ghosts*. Ralph

Richardson played 610 performances of a play called *Yellow Sand*s in 1926. But it was in 1925, John Barrymore recalled, remembering all the activities of the first evening he ever spent on the Haymarket's fabled stage:

"I waited until the theatre had become dark and empty. Then I walked out on stage, stood there, alone, looking toward the black vacuum of pit and stalls, and I knew what the Viscount St. Alban meant when he said that the poets had made Fame a monster . . . I might have quit that same night, had it not been for the sake of Winston Churchill. He was so fond of our family, such a great friend, that I didn't want to let him down."

Offstage in London, Barrymore loved walking through fogs and "felt they were full of romance and adventure." As Barrymore's friend Constance Collier told author Gene Fowler for his biography of the great thespian, "Whenever there was a real fog, Jack was in his element. He became most poetic . . . with his collar turned up and his hat pulled down over his brow as he tramped along in the heavy fog by the railings of Hyde Park."

One of the great traditions of London hotels is for the managers to leave hand-written notes for guests. Here's one from Simon Galic, Deputy General Manager of the Haymarket Hotel: "Dear Mr. Morehouse, A very warm welcome to the Haymarket. It's a pleasure having you stay with us. Regards, Simon."

As a result of my play, *Gangplank*, co-written with Mark Druck, Broadway and London producer David Garfinkle told me about staying at the Haymarket. He once patronized the hotel on my recommendation. "I love the swimming pool," David smiled. David was producing a musical version of the cult movie, *Ghost*, with Demi Moore, Patrick Swayze (who tragically passed away in 2009) and Whoopi Goldberg, on London's West End. Another thing he liked about the Haymarket was its location next to the Haymarket Theatre in the epicenter of the thriving West End.

The Haymarket Hotel, along with its sister hotels, has obviously been a labor of love for owners Tim and Kit Kemp. Kit as design director has poured herself into the decoration of the hotel with its fresh take on English design combined with quirky modern artwork; she defines her style as "English eccentric." Kit in 2008, according to the Firm-dale website, "won the prestigious Andrew Martin International Interior Designer of the Year award. Selected from a shortlist of designers by a celebrity panel including Thandie Newton, Twiggy and GQ Editor Dylan Jones, Kit Kemp was chosen for her distinctive interpretation of a quintessentially English style. Martin Waller says: 'Kit Kemp has redefined the concept of the city hotel. Her unique perspective brings a flamboyance to interior design without ever sacrificing the essential commandment of comfort.'" Labeled "the Oscars of the interior design world" the awards were set up in 1996 in order to discover and celebrate the talents of the world's best designers.

More about the reclusive Kemps can be gleaned from an article that appeared in *The Boston Post* by Christine Temin. I learned, in fact, a number of fascinating things about the Haymarket and its renowned designer from this jaunty newspaper item.

It seems that designer Kit Kemp has been quite prolific in her career. She has designed dozens and dozens of hotel bedrooms by now. She also has a charming design signature — the figure of a female man-nequin, which stands in the room sharing the same fabric which can be seen nearby, from the curtains to the valance to the cushions.

Of course there was the one time when this rather whimsical touch had an unexpected consequence. It seems one hotel guest, exhausted from her day's itinerary, returned to her room, draped her coat over the obliging female mannequin and promptly dropped off to sleep. Some time later she awoke, spotted the strange figure in her room and nearly lost it.

Kit Thomas got her start in the biz in the mid Eighties. At the time she was working for an architect when she had the great good personal and professional fortune to run into Tim Kemp, who was making his own living by transforming old buildings into youth hostels. The two like-minded youngsters got hitched and soon after opened their first ho-tel. Other young couples get married (or sometimes not) and like to visit hotels. Not Kit and Tim. They had to start their own. And their initial effort was Dorset Square, which had been a Regency-era townhouse before they got hold of it. The newlyweds turned the property into a splendidly elegant 38-room hotel in English country house style.

That was then. Now the two are a sort of chummy conglomerate, heading a $20 million dollar a year hotel empire with half a dozen small hotels and about as many restaurants scattered about London. Critics now give them credit for being in the vanguard of what's now known as "boutique" hotels, those smaller, fun places to stay. Kit recounts another amusing story about the time she had a devil of a time getting herself and her three casually dressed daughters seated in the restaurant of one of those non-boutique behemoth hotels. It was breakfast and the maitre d' insisted that her girls be "properly attired." Eventually a détente was worked out and they were placed at a table behind a voluminous potted plant. It made Kit realize that there just might be some room in the London hotel market for a place where a mother and her children might be served breakfast while wearing polo shirts.

Hence, you can wear pretty much whatever you want at a Kemp hotel. Even the owners can be spotted in jeans sauntering about their own premises. Which is not to say that their hotels are any less chic than the tony uptown joints. Just less strict. At least that's how many of their regulars seem to feel, including such not un-stylish folk like designer Isaac Mizrahi, actor Albert Finney, model Naomi Campbell, rock star Sting, and comic and actor Steve Martin.

Almost from the start, though, both the Covent Garden and its younger sibling the Charlotte Street Hotel have attracted a stellar show-biz crowd. After all, they wear a lot of silk sport coats in Hollywood, but not that many ties. It's often hot there, you know. This affinity for the entertainment industry types shouldn't be a surprise, considering that both hotels offer state-of-the-art screening rooms fitted out with Italian leather recliners.

Charlotte Street even started something they call their "Sunday Night Film Club," which for many guests has provided them with something to do in London on that otherwise low-key night (when many theatres and restaurants are closed). Moreover, this club is open to one and all. For about $40 you're served a three-course meal at the hotel's restaurant, after which you saunter down to the swanky screening room to watch a tastefully selected film. For instance, Kit Kemp has proudly noted, they screened *Chocolat* before its general release. How's that for a nice dessert after dinner?

But these hotels have many swell "touches." Like the "honesty" bar, where you pay for your drinks on the honor (or honour) system. That is, you run a tab and pay the reckoning when you check out. Isn't it flattering to be trusted, for once?

"A hotel should be a haven," Kit Kemp avers. How true. "When guests move the furniture around, we pay attention to what they've done to make the room more comfortable for themselves."

Ms. Kemp also strongly feels that "hotel interiors should be amusing. I do think some of them get so incredibly serious." I'm not so sure about this as a general maxim, but it does work wonderfully as a philosophy at her hotels. In addition to the mannequin motif, Kit Kemp hotel bedrooms have also been known to contain a jockey's weighing station, antique telephones and walls painted to look like wood. Even the artwork hanging on the walls is not your usual hotel landscape and still life. One room features a portrait of a hefty farmer's daughter who looks about to burp, or given her voluminous dimensions, about to erupt.

The rates at Firmdale hotels can also be less severe, though not exactly inexpensive. For instance, you'd be hard-pressed to find one of their rooms going for less than $200 a night, and the rates can rise to The Savoy — like $600-700 per evening. Though if you go to Knightsbridge, which is their hotel near Harrod's, you can get in the door for under $150. And your room will still have linens by Frette and toiletries by Miller Harris. The Knightsbridge may not have the exhaustive room-service that the big hotels can provide, but as long as you don't require a three-star meal in your room at three in the morning, you should be quite comfortable.

Although I only toured the Covent Garden Hotel, I immediately felt its kinship with the other Firmdale Hotels. The www.firmdale.com website details the new restaurant and bar at the Covent Garden Hotel which, I was informed, had recently undergone a makeover.

The revamped eatery got not only a separate bar area, but a longer pewter bar. Many a British pub offers pewter mugs, but an entire pewter bar? Incredible. The menu also was revamped with a new emphasis on what they call "British brasserie style cuisine." What this means, among other things, is that there's more fresh, seasonal produce on hand. You have an excellent choice of wines, by the glass, and the restaurant is open all day for the three traditional meals as well as for coffee, cocktails, and afternoon tea. Also worth noting are two private event rooms, easily adaptable to serve any function from a chic dining space to a formal corporate boardroom.

According to the website, afternoon tea is "the new power breakfast." Not exactly sure how that works out, unless you're prone to taking very late breakfasts, but I'm sure they know their business. In any event, power hungry or merely peckish for a scone, you can partake at either the "sumptuous drawing room" at the Charlotte Street Hotel, or in the sun-splashed "leafy garden" at Number Sixteen. Over at the Haymarket Hotel, however, you can enjoy a stylish Afternoon Tea for £25 or a truly indulgent Champagne Afternoon Tea for £33. Go a different direction and enjoy Cocktails & Canapés for two (£50) as a glamorous way to start the evening.

Any one of those sounds like it would fit me to a T. But I'm afraid we must be getting along to the next stop on this most luxurious of lines, with a visit to the Northbank of the River Thames.

THE SAVOY HOTEL

"The evening was dream-like. It began with an extraordinary Japanese dinner with Chairman Kwek at the Shogun Restaurant in Mayfair. My driver whisked me across London to the movie premier of Christian Carroll's *Suicide or Lulu and Me in a World Made for Two,* in which I played the voice of Louise Brooks. After the screening, the film director joined us at The Savoy for drinks. Entering the Thames Foyer is enchanting ... I walk through archways in the front hall and feel a lavish soul from the walls of London's 1889 landmark. Approaching what looks like a great birdcage — a winter garden gazebo — I enter a grand tearoom. It's filled with light, pouring from a circular dome of stained glass in the ceiling. Surrounded by chandeliers, flowers, music and portraits of legendary artists gave our film premier celebration at The Savoy an elegant-magic."

—Katherine Boynton

Jennifer Fox, President of Fairmont Hotels and Resorts, proudly hailed Fairmont hotels. "The Savoy was a favorite of Winston Churchill. In New York, Fairmont boasts The Plaza and in Quebec, Canada, the Chateau Frontenac," she explained.

"I can tell you that you'll feel like Churchill and start a little to assume some of his brilliance just stepping into The Savoy. In one sense, it has nothing to do with ambiance or décor and everything to do with making you feel special," Fox told *Elite*

Traveler Magazine. But a half billion dollar renovation has helped.

"As transatlantic travel became more popular in the early 1900s, many American Bars opened throughout London," Fox continued. "The American Bar at The Savoy is the longest surviving one of these bars and one of the most iconic cocktail bars in the world. Of course, stepping into the world renowned American Bar, you may feel like George Gershwin himself. Gershwin's 'Rhapsody in Blue' premiered here.

"In 1903 the first truly 'famous' bartender arrived at The American Bar, a lady named Ada 'Coley' Coleman, whose signature cocktail was the Hanky Panky, still a popular choice today. Ada's successor was the inspirational Harry Craddock, who not only created a number of classic cocktails but who notoriously compiled these recipes into the legendary *The Savoy Cocktail Book*, still regarded today as the bartender's bible."

The luxury of a stay at The Savoy now begins before you even check in. Book a Family Suite and enjoy The Savoy Suite Welcome. This package includes:

- Accommodation in a Family Suite and above
- Complimentary chauffeured car service with return airport/ station transfers
- Dedicated 24-hour butler service
- Welcome beverage
- Pressing of one garment per person per stay
- Rates start from £930 per night inclusive of VAT [as of 2014],

And for that, you can stay in one of the greatest luxury places on earth—a Savoy Suite.

Savoy Grill is without doubt one of London's most legendary restaurants. Frequented by celebrated diners such as Sir Winston Churchill, taurants. Frequented by celebrated diners such as Sir Winston Churchill, Oscar Wilde, Frank Sinatra, and HM Queen Elizabeth The Queen Mother, the original seating plan has been brought back for its reopening.

Jennifer Fox also said that while the "footprint" of Canadian-based Fairmont Hotels and Resorts leans toward North America, its future is pinned to the Middle East and Asia.

I stayed at The Savoy three times in cavernous riverfront (Thames-front) suites. The first time was in 1987 after my play, *The Actors*, had a long and successful run Off Broadway. The second was 2002 when my son Will was a young boy. The third was in 2006 after my book, *Inside New York's Grand Hotels*, was published. I can at least partly claim The Savoy is a home away from home for my family. My father stayed here starting in the 1920s.

If The Lanesborough Hotel, in the words of internationally renowned interior designer Trisha Williams, makes her feel as close to royalty as she may ever get, The Savoy is "home" to me. Part of it is like The Plaza Hotel; it's where my father stayed so long. In reality in terms of time spent at one place it, along with The Plaza, were really the places he spent the longest time. At a party he threw just before the making of *The African Queen*, one guest told Humphrey Bogart Africa was no place to take a lady, Lauren Bacall. "She's going, pal." "But," the guest interjected. "She's going." "Bogart and Ward liked each other," said Rebecca Morehouse, who is my stepmother and was married to my father, Ward Morehouse, for seventeen years. Bogart and my father had known each other since the Twenties, when Bogart was on Broadway in those fairly vacuous "Tennis anyone?" roles. Bogart was then in my father's movie, *Big City Blues*, before landing the role of gangster Duke Mantee in *The Petrified Forest*. (He repeated the role in the movie at the urging of star Leslie Howard, who would not do the movie version otherwise.) Bogart, of course, had been best known in his early career playing tough gangsters. He once admitted, Ezra Goodman reports in his book, *The Fifty-Year Decline and Fall of Hollywood*, that "physically, I'm not tough. I may think tough. I would say I'm kinda tough and calloused inside. I could use a foot more in height and fifty more pounds and fifteen years off my age and then God help all you." Goodman quotes Bogey's wife, Lauren Bacall, as saying Bogart's face looked "as if somebody'd stepped on it." Goodman in the same book calls Bacall "a sort of Humphrey Bogart in skirts." Bogart was dramatic and so was my father.

Just as you cannot separate celebrities, authors, playwrights and actors from London's hotels, it's hard to separate the shop-lined broad avenues and quaint byways of Mayfair, The Strand, Piccadilly and Covent Garden from the finest of hotels. It's as if they are part of the stage setting. So the Omega store in its own way is as much a part of nearby Brown's as are Kipling and Lindbergh who stayed at the hotel.

Tallulah Bankhead lived in a townhouse on Farm Street in the West End. When my father interviewed her there her love bird "Gaylord" was perched nearby. The interview was a bit disconcerting for him as Bankhead, like Marilyn Monroe after her, seldom wore underwear. She once proclaimed she "was as pure as the driven slush." Mae West famously said she was once Snow White — but just drifted!

No one quite ever described shopping in London quite like the late singer Rudy Vallee. In his book, *My Time Is Your Time*, the name of his theme song, he says London is a shopper's delight. Vallee started as a musician and singer in bands, then graduated to radio, then became Number 1 — for a while. In the 1960s he had a huge comeback starring in the Broadway musical, *How to Succeed in Business Without Really Trying*. Vallee, who was at the time playing saxophone at The Savoy Hotel, wrote, "Any time I could seize a moment off from the saxophonic chores, I would frequent the shops along Bond Street which catered to the sartorial needs of the man. As far as clothes are concerned (and in many other ways . . .), England is a man's country. . . . I amassed a collection of around two hundred pairs of socks, about two hundred and fifty ties, suits and coats tailored with Chesterfield style, then in vogue." Sounds like Rudy could have given even César Ritz a run for his money in the clothes horse stakes.

Vallee writes of his Savoy experience, "I played every evening: upstairs in the beautiful, pillared, red-carpeted main dining room, where dined such personalities as Tetrazzini, Marconi (who lived for a time at the Seville Hotel in New York; The Seville is now The Carlton), Fokker, the German aircraft inventor, diplomats, artists, actors, etc.; and early in the morning downstairs in the large ballroom with its floor set on springs, playing opposite the large Savoy Orpheans, a band of some twenty-two pieces which rivaled Paul Whiteman's aggregation in its brilliance and beauty of tone."

Vallee had been persuaded to remain in London longer than he originally anticipated to get a "royal appointment" to teach the Prince of Wales to play the sax. "I could not wait for the Prince's return from Africa so I might become the regal saxophone tutor," Vallee added.

The Savoy opened in 1889, after the success of The Savoy Theatre where Richard D'Oyly Carte stepped out onto the 27-foot deep stage, dwarfed by the 30-foot high proscenium arch and smashed a glowing electric light bulb as black-tie audience members gasped. They had just witnessed a performance of Gilbert and Sullivan's comic opera *Patience* and the impresario wanted to demonstrate the safety of the newfangled electric light bulb. The theater, unlike the venerable Haymarket or smaller Comic Opera Theatres and their neighbors, was the first London theater to be lit entirely by electricity. The gold, satin curtain behind him shimmered in the reflection of 1200 incandescent bulbs, and gaslights were — except on those rare occasions when the 120-horse power generator conked out — history. *Iolanthe, The Mikado, The Gondoliers*, and other shows premiered at the Theatre. When The Savoy Hotel itself premiered eight years later, the Theatre's entrance was moved to the hotel's courtyard off The Strand where it remains today.

The Savoy compiled some history and, for accuracy's sake, I give it to you more-or-less verbatim:

The Savoy opened its doors to an eager public in 1889, the brainchild of the Gilbert and Sullivan impresario Richard D'Oyly Carte. Built on the site of a former palace, the hotel took five years and vast expenses to complete and incorporated unheard of features, including full electric lighting and what for the time was a startling number of baths: 67 in total. Richard D'Oyly

Carte had laid the foundations for The Savoy's heritage — British style and tradition coupled with innovation.

Masterful timing resulted in a glittering first season and D'Oyly Carte ensured The Savoy's continued success by employing celebrated Swiss hotelier César Ritz to be its Manager, accompanied by Maître Chef Auguste Escoffier, and Louis Echenard, a master of wine, as Maître d'hotel. Other notables over the years who had "Savoy" on their resume included Guccio Gucci, who began his professional life at the hotel — as a dishwasher, and Harry Craddock, Head Barman of the American Bar, who helped create cocktail culture in London.

Escoffier created dishes for Sarah Bernhardt, Lily Langtry, Dame Nellie Melba and the Prince of Wales, later Edward VII; Ritz instituted the impeccable service, attention to detail, and creativity that came to be the hallmark of the hotel.

In the ensuing years the hotel saw numerous expansions, always incorporating the latest amenities and facilities and a degree of self-sufficiency. The Savoy would not rely on the vagaries of the outside world for power or water, or indeed for roasted coffee.

The Savoy has always sparkled with glittering parties. One of the most famous was the Gondola dinner, hosted by Champagne millionaire and Wall Street financier George Kessler, in July 1905. Venice was recreated in the old forecourt, lit by 400 Venetian lamps. The centerpiece was a silk-lined gondola decorated with 12,000 fresh carnations. There was a baby elephant, a five-foot birthday cake and arias sung by the tenor Caruso, who was paid £450.

From these very lavish early beginnings to the present day, The Savoy has played host to London's most talked about gatherings. The Savoy has hosted the South Bank Show Awards and Evening Standard Film Awards. The hotel is also proud to be hotel sponsor and host of the pre-party event for the BAFTA Television Awards. Other events of note at the hotel include the

Wimbledon Ball and the announcement of the Samuel Johnson Book Awards.

In 1923 the two Savoy dance bands, The Savoy Orpheans and The Savoy Havana Band, became the first to broadcast regularly from a hotel. The BBC's "Dance Music from The Savoy Hotel in London" was broadcast to millions worldwide. In the Ballroom Gershwin gave London its first performance of "Rhapsody in Blue" and Carroll Gibbons played nightly. Today, the Thames Foyer, where Strauss conducted, Caruso sang and Pavlova danced in cabaret, continues to feature live music, with a resident piano player tickling the ivories during Afternoon Tea service and evening cocktail hour.

Always a magnet for the well known and well heeled, by 1914 the hotel and the Savoy Grill had established itself as a rendezvous for leading stars, impresarios and critics. Royalty patronized The Savoy in such numbers that the special bell heralding their arrival had to be abandoned.

From the end of the First World War into the Thirties, Maharajas took up residence with glittering retinues, Pavlova danced, the Archbishop of Canterbury attended the cabaret. Eccentricities were catered for without hesitation, including opera singer Luisa Tetrazzini's crocodile!

Winston Churchill was a famously devoted Savoyard. He visited The Savoy every week when he was in London and was present at the great occasion when Mrs. Eleanor Roosevelt was the guest of honor of the Pilgrim Society. The restaurant was closed to the public and a thousand guests attended, including the newly-married Princess Elizabeth and Prince Philip. Other famous newlyweds to visit The Savoy included Elizabeth Taylor and first husband Nicky Hilton, who celebrated their honeymoon here.

Past stars of the silver screen such as Cary Grant, James Stewart, Frank Sinatra, Gene Kelly, Fred Astaire, Katharine Hepburn and Laurence Olivier and recent celebrity guests including Catherine Zeta-Jones and Michael Douglas, Robert De Niro and

Pamela Anderson have long been attracted to The Savoy's Art Deco glamour and understated elegance. The connection with Hollywood continues as the hotel has played "leading lady" in a number of recent movies, including *Notting Hill, Entrapment* and *Dirty Pretty Things.*

Now proudly a Fairmont Hotel, the 263-room Savoy offers 19,000 square feet of distinctive function space, stunning Thames views and an incomparable location steps from Covent Garden, the West End theaters, Trafalgar Square and the City financial district. Its famous features include the Michelin-starred Savoy Grill, the American Bar, and one of two rooftop pools in the city. In January 2005, The Savoy was noted on both the "Condé Nast *Traveler* Gold List" and the *"Travel + Leisure 500"* alongside other celebrated Fairmont Hotels and Resorts.

Quite a history. Though I can't help wondering if Pavlova actually danced with the Archbishop of Canterbury at that cabaret. And what was a Hilton doing staying at The Savoy? Miss Taylor may have had something to do with that.

Nor were Taylor-Hilton the first power Hollywood couple to grace the hotel. Vivien Leigh and Laurence Olivier first met there in their lustrous youth, before their international fame in Hollywood, before Nazi bombs hit The Savoy and destroyed some of the fanciful London churches and other landmarks they loved and killed nearly 30,000 Londoners.

The Thames sparkled in the moonlight as Big Ben solemnly stood guard upriver. It was 11:45 p.m., fashionable time in London town to have dinner at The Savoy. Seated only a few tables apart were two actors destined to change the history of romance as well as theater and film. Vivien Leigh and Laurence Olivier. Olivier looked at her and not only beheld one of the most beautiful women he had ever seen but felt a connection he didn't fully understand. Here were two people, beautiful and talented to an extreme, thrown momentarily together. He had recently seen her in her first London success, *The Mask of Virtue,* which even the sternest newspaper critics had praised her performance in. But despite his proximity to the stage, it was not at all the same as viewing her in The Savoy's candlelit River Terrace.

The two did not actually meet until she went backstage to see him in a production of *Romeo and Juliet* in which Olivier and John Gielgud alternately played the roles of the romantic Romeo and dashing Mercutio at the Theatre Royal. "She decided to go backstage to congratulate him on his performance in *Romeo and Juliet*," writes Anne Edwards in her biography of Vivien Leigh, *Vivien Leigh*. "There were a few people in his dressing room when she arrived, but he was aware of her presence as soon as she entered. He asked her courteously if she had any theater plans after telling her he had seen her in *The Mask of Virtue* and had been impressed with her ability."

"'I'm Vivien Leigh, and I just had to tell you how marvelous you were,'" she told Olivier. He thought, Edwards says, she was the most beautiful woman he had ever seen and he asked her to lunch with him to discuss her own theatrical plans.

She told him she had been offered the part in a play called *The Happy Hypocrite* opposite Ivor Novello, who had been compared to Noël Coward and was, at the time, a kind of English theater's answer to a young John Barrymore. Olivier suggested she take the role and at that very moment became her mentor.

During World War II, Alec Guinness in his book *Blessings in Disguise* says just how magnetic Vivien Leigh could be even to total strangers. While stationed in North Africa, Leigh, who was touring in a pre-Northern African invasion play, tried to get Guinness and a fellow officer a ride back to their ship.

"She button-holed, with all her wheedling charm, a starry-eyed Admiral," he wrote. "Caressing the lapels of his uniform, admiring his campaign ribbons, she suddenly asked him what he was doing for the next few hours. His eyes danced with excitement as he blushingly replied, 'Nothing!'

"'Then,' Vivien went on, 'you won't be needing your car. . . . I have two darling friends here, and they've simply got to be driven back to a little place.'"

My father once took the late Rebecca Morehouse, who worked for

The Atlanta Journal, Time and *Playbill*, to dinner with Vivien Leigh and Laurence Olivier one night at their place in Christ Church Street.

"Ward knew them, I did not," Rebecca said. "So I'm at table with Scarlett O'Hara and her celebrated, handsome actor-husband, the most famous couple in the world.

"They knew the pain of separation. He was on Broadway in a play when she was playing Scarlett in California. Her impatience to finish the picture was all about him, being with him. When they could arrange it, it wasn't easy, they got on planes and met in the middle of the country, some place with an airport, where didn't matter. 'We did terrible things all over your beautiful country,' Vivien said cheerfully, with no apparent regret."

Long after the famous thespian twosome divorced, my father visited Leigh in her dressing room when she was appearing in *Duel of Angels,* her last play on Broadway. On her dressing table, in a silver frame, was a photo of "Larry."

The Savoy is also the story of a thousand and one tales of wayfarers who have fallen in love like Vivien Leigh, although often without similar notoriety.

Even Big Ben, however, may have swing-and-swayed ever so slightly to the strains of The Savoy Ballroom of the London premier of George Gershwin's "Rhapsody in Blue." No stranger to the most popular of music, the BBC's Prince of Music was broadcast from The Savoy Hotel to millions around the globe.

Greer Garson is best known to American movie audiences as the courageous British wife and mom during the early days of World War II in the film *Mrs. Miniver.* That heartfelt epic of Greer and her family coping with the Nazi bombing and Dunkirk, released in 1942, just as America was entering the war, may have done as much to boost support for the war cause in the States as Edward R. Murrow's dramatic radio reports from a battered London. But Miniver was not Ms. Garson's introduction to Hollywood. That historic occasion took place years earlier in the British capital.

One evening, Hollywood mogul Louis B. Mayer was so enchanted with Greer Garson's innocent beauty in a mediocre melodrama playing at the St. James Theatre by the name of *Old Music* that he invited her for supper at the Savoy Grill after her performance. Already aware of Mayer's predilection for "discovering" Hollywood's next major star only after accepting his romantic overtures, Garson raced home, changed into more demure clothes, and persuaded her mother to come along to the Savoy Grill. Greer must have put on a good performance because she landed a $500-a-week contract — Mayer's opening gambit with a lot of his lady stars — and soon after reported to the West Coast, though to little if any work at first. When she later retreated to London to make *Goodbye Mr. Chips*, playing the dying wife, she was nominated for an Oscar and returned to America an international star.

My own show business experience in London is so far limited to presenting that American rock singer named EJ in several venues including the famous military "In and Out Club" on St. James Square (and which once served duty as Nancy Astor's townhouse). She was quite a hit with those who assembled in the great hall, which had once been Lady Astor's dining room. Later in the evening, she serenaded some of the admirals who were the backbone of the club's membership. Another high point was getting her to sing several Cole Porter shows in The Savoy's American Bar even though piano music, and not singers, was the room's music staple. These were small personal triumphs set against the larger hope of seeing the musical I helped co-write the book for produced on the West End.

The *New York Times* liked *The Actors*, then a production of my play, *My Four Mothers*, was packed at Jan Hus Theatre. Coming to The Savoy the winter of the same year opened up the idea that I would actually make it as a successful playwright. A few years later I penned a book on The Waldorf-Astoria that would propel me into the world of great hotels and their history of which the book on London hotels is the culmination.

That jaunt promoting an American rock singer in 2005 may have been the most unusual as I was accompanied by three friends of hers as well. They stayed in one room of the suite; I in the other. I went to bed early; they reemerged from the clubs they had visited late and I was relieved that they were safe if not entirely sound and probably more than a little high. But, perhaps, my best productive effort in London was introducing EJ to the handsome young journalist who became her boyfriend.

But really all my experiences at The Savoy have been both wonderful and unusual. I first stayed there after my play, The Actors, had been quite a success Off-Broadway. It had run for a total of nine months, closing in April of 1987. That same year, I got an agent to produce one other play, *My Four Mothers*, Off-Broadway.

I recently stayed in Cape May at New Jersey's Congress Hall Hotel, introduced nearly 200 years ago in 1816, where a number of Presidents, including Ulysses S. Grant, stayed. "We are definitely not pet friendly," said an otherwise solicitous member of the Congress Hall staff. They would have been put out, to say the least, if they had encountered opera diva Luisa Tetrazzini's pet crocodile, which The Savoy accommodated with aplomb. (Turkey Tetrazzini, in case you were wondering, was named after the Tetrazzinis.)

The time is 1933. My father wanted a holiday, one in which he could enjoy theater without writing about it for once. Here's his report, which talks about The Savoy, where he always stayed, and The Savoy Grill, which was virtually an office for many then-famous Broadway players.

"London plays seemed better. Or perhaps it was because I was just seeing them, and not seeing them to write about them. I was taking a leave of absence from *The Sun* and it was my first time abroad without copy to write. For the New York playgoer, wandering about the stalls of West End, things have to be awfully just-so, if he is to like the London theater at all. It's much easier to take if you're relaxed. *The Lake*, as played by such people as Marie Nye and May Whitty, appeared to be good drama. Raymond Massey gave a strong performance in a spurious war piece called *The Ace*. Gielgud was in the beautiful but ponderous *Richard of Bordeaux*. Mary Ellis, with something of a West End following, was trying *Music in the Air* and Ivor Novello, as prolific as Noël Coward, but without Noël's talent, was doing his latest comedy. I've forgotten the title. That, in itself, is significant. It must have been no play at all. For I have always thought

91

that I could remember the title of every play, the name of every actor; that I could, without a miss, go through the personnel of the Daniel Frohman Lyceum stock company or the full roster of the original theater in John Street.

Gilbert Miller, who is a polished producer as well as a linguist and an aviator, and who is becoming, more and more, a showman of the London theater with a branch office in New York, was seldom out of the Savoy Grill during that London week. Neither was Kitty Miller, nor Francine Larrimore, Adrianne Allen, Guy Bolton, Florence Britton, Romney Brent, Basil Sidney. Or Dennis King, my old friend from the Utah airways. Marc Connelly, whose stock as a dramatist took a sharp rise with the writing of the beautiful *Green Pastures*, gave the best of the week's parties, an affair for Ray Massey held in the Pinafore room of The Savoy. Massey was congratulated on his work in *The Ace*. "Great!" everybody said. But he wasn't happy about it. He knew it wasn't much of a play and he didn't feel that he was giving anything beyond a routine performance. He was really getting discouraged about acting anyway. He'd begun to think that he'd have to go in for direction entirely. Some of his friends had been urging him to do Shakespeare; there were others who thought he ought to play Abraham Lincoln, realizing that he could look like Lincoln and that he'd had life-long interest in Lincoln as a character. But how was Ray Massey then to know that Robert E. Sherwood was to come along five years later with a play that would give him the great rôle of his career?

I bade Marc Connelly goodbye after that Pinafore room party, and told him I'd see him in New York. Two days later we found ourselves at adjoining tables in The Ritz bar, Paris. These Americans do get around!"

LANGHAM HOTEL

The Langham was London's first grand hotel when it opened in 1865. His Royal Highness The Prince of Wales presided over the opening ceremony.

A former civil war union officer, James Sanderson, who is believed to have written the first cookbook for an army, became the Langham's first general manager. The hotel is now the flagship property of the Hong Kong-based Langham Hotels International. It has 380 rooms.

The dazzling new Palm Court is where the tradition of afternoon tea was born 130 years ago.

We enjoyed tea with Duncan Palmer, the general manager, who is also an expert on the kinds of managers running grand hotels today. "I would say there's more of an international set among the general managers of all London hotels. Asia has come up for the last twenty or thirty years. When I worked as general manager of the Oriental Hotel in Bangkok, we had a staff of 1200 for a 400-bedroom hotel — a ratio of three to one — whereas today here at the Langham we have one point two to one." Prior to becoming general manager of the Langham, he was general manager of the Sukhothai Hotel in Bangkok. Mr. Palmer also worked as general manager of The Savoy in London for three years. His career includes twelve years with the Mandarin Oriental Group throughout Asia, including Macau, Manila, Bangkok and Jakarta.

"I have the most wonderful opportunity to work with the owners and management team I have appointed … to reestablish the Langham Hotel as one of the most popular, luxurious and service-oriented hotels in London."

In 1889, nearly a quarter century after the Langham first opened, Joseph Marshall Stoddart commissioned Oscar Wilde and Arthur Conan Doyle to write stories for *Lippincott's Monthly Magazine*. Both stories were published in the magazine the following year. They are among the most famous in British literary history. Wilde wrote "The Picture of Dorian Gray" and Conan Doyle "The Sign of the Four." Besides Oscar Wilde and Conan Doyle, other notable guests included Noël Coward and Guy Burgess.

In 2010 a plaque commemorating the 1889 meeting between Oscar Wilde, Arthur Conan Doyle and Joseph Stoddart was unveiled.

During World War II the hotel was used by the army, damaged during the German Blitz, and forced to close. The British Broadcasting Corporation used the hotel as satellite offices after the war, and the hotel reopened in 1991 as the Langham Hilton after being refurbished.

The hotel was featured in the James Bond film, *Golden Eye*, in 1995. The exterior was filmed at the hotel but the interior shots were done in a studio. The hotel was also featured in Michael Winterbottom's 1999 film, *Wonderland,* and in the 2006 film, *Garfield: A Tale of Two Kitties.* It was also featured in Mary Kate and Ashley Olsen's TV movie, *Winning London.*

Mr. Palmer continues,

"In the 1860s Chinese architecture was influencing European architecture up to a point. My owner being Chinese, we have quite a few Chinese amenities in the hotel.

"That's what business we're in, in hotels, we're in the theater business. We're entertaining our guests. We're on stage.

QUEEN MARY 2

The largest ship in the world could also be called the grandest hotel on water. We spent an elegant eight days crossing the Atlantic Ocean to return home from England to New York City on the Queen Mary 2. One passenger described it as "arriving in style." They have many formal nights where one dresses for dinner so be sure to bring at least a couple of gowns or suites. Tuxedos are welcome. Here you'll find a cultured crowd and activities carefully planned by the entertainment director catering to a variety of tastes. Entertainment includes top artists performing in concerts, musical reviews and even Shakespearean plays. We caught the Royal Academy of Dramatic Arts' vibrant adaptation of *The Merchant of Venice,* an exquisite planetarium show taking us into space narrated by Lawrence Fishburn, and many movie nights on the big screen. One can take classes like ballroom dance, painting, internet, wine tasting, and culinary classes. A whole library, duty-free shopping, English teas complete with scones and clotted crème, masquerade balls, casinos, a luxurious spa with beauty treatments, a gym which looks out onto the ocean, pools, saunas, Jacuzzi's. Loving childcare is provided to give parents a break. If traveling with your dog, there is even a kennel that allows you to visit your furry friend and also socialize with other like-minded owners and their dogs. The Queen Mary 2 is full of opportunities to learn, relax and have quality entertainment.

"The food on the Queen Mary 2 is incredibly fresh and deliciously prepared. Todd English was one restaurant that was a privilege to dine in, serving delicious Mediterranean food presented with creativity and new combinations. We also frequently had dinner at The Britannia, which we loved as they changed their menu every night, keeping it fresh and interesting. The head chef went the extra mile, always having vegetarian options or being flexible and willing to adapt to requests ... even if not on the menu! A special feature of this restaurant was that we were seated with two other couples and were delighted to make new friends on our travels. If you feel like a more casual evening or meal, you can still eat like royalty all day long in The Kings Court. They will also have options in the Chefs Gallery nearby where food from different countries is served. I had a delicious Malaysian soup where I got to choose the ingredients to put in... or a Mexican day where similarly we made our own tacos. Although not representing a country, I was especially excited about Chocolate Day where they had ice sculptures and tables filled with chocolate desserts.

"One may think this is too tempting a setup for those wishing to lose weight, but I found that after the first day of seeing the extravaganza of endless choices, when there's so much available, you only take what you really need. After all, there are over 2,000 passengers so they do need to be prepared. And this staff of over 1,000 is! They deliver a quality service that's off the charts. One standout was Analisa, who made up our room every day. She always had a smile and greeted me with a joy-filled "hello" or "good morning." Seeing her in the hallway filled it with a light I will never forget. It's the special people like Analisa that fill the Queen Mary 2 with love.

"Everyone will have a different favorite part of the Queen Mary 2. For me a great highlight was jogging every morning around the ship on Deck 7. Here I had infinite views of the sea and caught glimpses of rainbows, happy dolphins, and the spray of great whales!

"The Queen Mary 2 across the board brings quality with a capital 'Q'."

—Katherine Boynton

It's interesting to note that with the endless food available many people don't overeat. Executive Chef Klaus Kremer says, "After two or three days, people start reducing. They say to themselves, 'If I go on like that for another six days, you're going to roll me off.' So after the first two or three days, they're reducing themselves already saying, 'I can't go on like that.'"

What about training the food staff, we asked? "Whoever is here is already trained. The basic training is done. We have a lot of Filipino and Indian chefs and most of them have been trained by a European chef."

One may wonder why the Queen Mary 2 is included in this book on London's Greatest Grand Hotels. There's a simple reason: the 1,132 feet (340 meters) long ship, with seventeen decks, is a floating hotel on water. Another criterion for being in this book is the passengers' or guests' ability to order anything at anytime, and the QM2 delivers this, just like the best hotels on land.

Kremer continues, "The first ship I was on was in October 1988, the *Vista Fjord*. I stayed there for six years. I'm 52, so half of my life I spent at sea and that was with Cunard."

> "I did my apprenticeships in Switzerland and Sweden in restaurants, and in 1988 I thought let's go for it, let's go to sea! I was lured by the thought of going around the world and working at the same time.
>
> "So you do two things at work, why not work and see the world at the same time. And Cunard actually bought the *Vista Fjord* and we went to Alaska. And it was the only Cunard ship that (at that time) went to Alaska.
>
> "I loved it. I did three years there. And then I went to the QE2. Eight years on the QE2. Nine years on the Queen Mary."

One of the chef's biggest thrills was sailing into Hamburg Harbour as 100,000 people watched.

We asked him if passenger preferences in food are affected by the weather. "In cold weather, people tend to eat more. But we are cooking lighter than we used to. We used to do a lot of heavy sauces. Not so much anymore." Observing the QM2's cavernous kitchen, it looked like the size of the grand hotel kitchen at The Waldorf-Astoria in New York. Klaus said, referring to the kitchen at The Brittania, "It's big and we need every bit of it. We have seventy waiters at one time on the food preparation tables and fifty chefs on the other side preparing the food."

At a time when many hotels around the world are cutting back on room service, here you'll never have to leave your room — morning, mid-day, or evening — for caviar, lobster or pizza.

The suites range in size from 335 to 2,249 square feet, the latter for the Grand Duplex. Besides the servers and food, the views from an outside cabin room are enough to make you feel like "the king of the world" to quote Leonardo DiCaprio's character in *Titanic.*

Although these grand ships are not homes for retirees, one woman found a way to retire in style. She found it more economical to book a small cabin on an around-the-world cruise on the QE2 than pay the costs of living in New York City.

Stepping aboard the Queen Mary 2 in Southampton on the afternoon of October 8th, 2014, we felt joined with a great legacy — the thousands of passengers who sailed in Cunard ships across the Atlantic ever since the 1,154-ton paddle steamer *Brittania* and its three sister ships, the *Arcadia, Caledonia* and *Columbia,* entered service.

In November of 2014, the Queen Mary 2 completed her 250th transatlantic crossing. Angus Struthers, Marketing Director for Cunard, said:

"2014 has been a fantastic year for Cunard with a highlight being the tenth birthday celebrations of our flagship Queen Mary 2. It's truly remarkable how she captures the hearts and attention wherever she goes — from her birthday call in Sydney to more than 2,050 joining the celebrations in Hamburg, to the arrival of the whole three-ship fleet in our home port of Southampton in May. We were delighted that His Royal Highness, The Duke of Edinburgh was able to join us on that day. It was really a fitting way to mark this special occasion for the grandest ocean liner ever built."

Once we were ensconced in our ocean view cabin, we hear the mellifluous voice of Captain Kevin Oprey welcoming us on the loudspeaker. In the daily program he elaborated that, "Cunard ships have spanned the mighty Atlantic Ocean since 1840, welcoming aboard those seeking adventure, style and sophistication."

According to Cunard Queen Mary 2's food statistics for a transatlantic crossing are:

Muesli	13,200 portions
Marmalade/Jam	7,560 portions
Butter	1,500 kg
Fresh Eggs	36,700 units
Herbs & Spices	55 kg
Potatoes	11,000 kg
Flour	2,950 kg
Rice	1,800 kg
Bananas	1,200 kg
Fresh Strawberries	550 kg
Tomatoes	1,600 kg
Beef	2,500 kg
Pork	2,950 kg
Lamb	500 kg
Sausages	1,270 kg
Duck	630 kg
Ham	690 kg
Fish	340 kg
Tea Bags	30,000 units
Coffee	560 kg
Non Alcoholic Drinks	9,210 units
Milk	7,000 litres
Champagne	370 bottles
Beer	7,860 bottles
Wine	2,350 bottles
Other Spirits	690 litres
Cigars	200 units
Cigarettes	3,200 packs

And everything is grand. With over 5,000 commissioned artworks in the Queen's public rooms, two of the most heralded are John McKenna's bronze relief mural in the Grand Lobby and Barbara Broekman's tapestry which depicts the superliner with its bridge and New York Harbor.

The QM2's launch in March 2003 was full of pomp and royalty!

Using the same scissors her mother had used to launch Queen Elizabeth in 1938 and her grandmother had used to launch Queen Mary in 1934, Queen Elizabeth cut the ribbon, releasing the bottle of wine which duly smashed onto the side of the newly-named liner. She then pressed the button that electrically released the launching rigger.

Nothing happened. For 70 seconds it seemed as if the ship did not move. Workmen high up on her deck leaned and shouted, "Give us a shove!" Shipyard director George Parker joined in the spirit of the request and bowler-hatted, he sprang to the bows and gave the liner a shove. He jubilantly waved his bowler when, by a coincidence, she began to move. In a little over two minutes after the Queen had named her, the new Elizabeth had slid smoothly into the Clyde. Newspapers the next day claimed the Queen had wept as the new ship entered the Clyde and that Prince Philip took a white handkerchief from his pocket and handed it to her.

The 178-seat Princess Grill, decorated in silver, is for guests in the Junior Suite staterooms. Both Grills offer single seating. Max Weissenhoffer, a Broadway and West End theater producer who owns six theaters in London, will often enjoy dining in the Queens Grill when he's aboard.

In addition, Queen Mary 2 offers several alternative dining venues. The 156-seat Todd English Restaurant on Deck 8 offers innovative Mediterranean cuisine in a modern setting. The room has been designed with intimate alcoves and architectural detailing and overlooks the Pool Terrace. The informal 478-seat King's Court serves breakfast and lunch buffet style. Decorated screens transform the area into different dining venues at night: La Piazza (Italian), Lotus (Asian), and Coriander (Indian). For snacks the Boardwalk Café offers fast food choices outdoors and the Golden Lion Pub offers traditional English pub food for lunch.

The Royal Court Theatre, with tiered seating for 1,094, is the location for the main entertainment of the evening with full-scale, West End-style productions as well as featured entertainers. Classically elegant in style, there is a hydraulic proscenium stage and highly sophisticated light and sound equipment as well as excellent sight lines.

Queen Mary 2's Queen Room is the largest ballroom at sea and is designed for ballroom dancing, cocktail parties, and afternoon teas. It features a dramatic high ceiling (more than seven meters high), crystal chandeliers, sweeping ocean views on both sides of the ship and the largest dance floor at sea (measuring 7.5 by 13 meters).

Illuminations acts as a cinema, lecture hall, and broadcast studio. Perhaps even more exciting is the fact that the room also hosts the first Planetarium aboard a ship.

"We're trying to have a mix of lectures," says a Cunard executive. "We'll have some really interesting intellectual speakers, be it science, be it astronomy lectures, but we also have best selling writers talking about their experiences as authors. We still like to have people like John Cleese because he is great value and great entertainment.

"We had that wonderful experience last year with James Taylor and his band. For people who experience James Taylor doing two concerts on the Queen Mary 2, that is what Cunard is all about.

"Another area that is evolving is the length of a transatlantic voyage. When ocean liners were the only way to cross the Atlantic, speed was very important to passengers, particularly to business travelers. In their heyday, liners could make the crossing in just under five days. With the advent of the jet airliner, speed is no longer as important. As a result, in the mid-1990s, Cunard increased the length of a crossing from five to six nights. This reduced fuel costs and gave the ship more flexibility to avoid storms. In 2010, Cunard introduced some seven-night crossings to Queen Mary 2's schedule."

This draws a clientele who is looking for an experience of leisurely travel with time to enjoy the ocean, a great library, new classes and culture, and some of the best food and entertainment anywhere.

You can see many stars aboard which may be well nigh impossible to see in London or New York's theaters. Sixteen-time Grammy Award winning musician Sting performed aboard the Queen Mary 2 on October 28, 2014. Among the songs he sang were ones from his Broadway musical, *The Last Ship*. Over the years fifteen Cunard ships were built in Wallsend in the northeast of England where Sting himself grew up.

Of course on such a leisurely sea cruise you can see many other stars, as well — the stars up in the night sky. After all, there's no place to really drink in the Milky Way like the middle of the Atlantic!

One link with tradition that occasionally is bothersome to voyage veterans is that the restaurant that one dines in is linked to the passenger's cabin category. Guests in the top suites aboard the QM2 dine in the Queens Grill; those in the other suites dine in the Princess Grill; while the vast majority of the passengers dine in the main dining room, the Brittania Restaurant. Some people perceive this as a perpetuation of the class system as seen in movies such as *Titanic*. "We don't have barriers up. Really, it is just the accommodations, the restaurant and the Queens Grill lounge, whereas everyone has access to the rest of the ship, be it Canyon Ranch, the theater and everything else. I think it works well onboard and we are not shy about it. But it is no different than getting onboard a British Airways plane and having economy class and first. It is no different than hotels that have exclusive bars and floors and suites," said a Cunard executive.

In fact, some of Cunard's competitors are introducing similar concepts on their ships. While flattered by the imitation, "I think other lines having some spa suites and separate restaurants doesn't quite capture the specialness of the Queens Grill and the Princess Grill," he said.

In May 2014 the Queen Mary 2 became the Cunard's flagship liner, after the QE2 relinquished its flagship title after being the longest serving Cunard flagship liner. The QM2 was also the first ocean liner to enter Cunard service in over 35 years. Since that maiden voyage in 2003, the ship, as of this writing, has sailed 1.5 million nautical miles on 430 voyages and stopped at 177 ports in 60 countries.

Whether the kingdom is on water or land, these London hotels have an extraordinary quality of sincere service that's inspiring to witness. You can see this service daily and even hourly at any of *London's Greatest Grand Hotels.*